Towards Evening

R

Towards Evening

Reflections on Aging, Illness, and the
Soul's Union with God

by Mary Hope
Edited by LaVonne Neff

PARACLETE PRESS
Brewster, Massachusetts

Library of Congress Cataloging-in-Publication Data

Hope, Mary, b. 1892.
    Towards evening: reflections on aging, illness, and the soul's union with God/by Mary Hope; edited by LaVonne Neff.
        p. cm.
    ISBN 1-55725-183-5 (pbk.)
    1. Aged—Religious life—Meditations. 2. Spirituality—Catholic Church. 3. Aging—Religious aspects—Christianity—Meditations. 4. Devotional calendars. I. Neff, LaVonne. II. Title.
BX2372.H6 1997
242'.65—DC21   97-628
                                                                          CIP

10 9 8 7 6 5 4 3 2 1

© 1997 by Paraclete Press
ISBN: 1-55725-183-5

Published by Paraclete Press
Brewster, Massachusetts
Printed in the United States of America

About *Towards Evening*

When *Towards Evening* was published by Sheed and Ward in 1955, the dust jacket identified Mary Hope only as "a lay woman, who has had much to do with the very old all her life." The book itself, which takes the form of a year's journal, reveals her as a Southern lady, a devout Catholic, a published writer, and caregiver to her aged aunt and mother. She was also, we learn from reading the entries, a well-connected world traveler. Much of her childhood was spent in Italy, France, and England (she received First Communion in Rome from Pope Pius X), and her family was on intimate terms with the renowned Cardinal Gibbons of Baltimore. Clearly Miss Hope was a woman of influence—one who, in the self-effacing fifties, would not have wanted her real name on a book of intimate spiritual musings.

In fact, the author of *Towards Evening* was Daisy Haywood Moseley. Born in Raleigh, North Carolina, in 1892, she moved with her family to Glen Ridge, New Jersey, as a child. A brother, James, was killed in World War I; another brother, Nicholas, taught at Yale. Miss Moseley, who earned a B.A. from the College of Notre Dame in Maryland and also studied at the New York School of Social Work, was the author of *Sunshine and Saints*, a collection of saints' biographies for young people (1935), and *Blessed Robert Southwell*, a biography of the sixteenth-century English martyr (1957). In addition, she frequently contributed articles to *Catholic World, Commonweal, Sign*, and other religious magazines. *Towards Evening* is her journal from 1949.

In 1959 Miss Moseley moved to Chapel Hill, North Carolina, remaining in her native state until her death twenty years later. Her correspondence, diaries, and other writings are in the Southern Historical Collection at the University of North Carolina, Chapel Hill.

Miss Moseley lived in a rich Catholic milieu, where saints' names were as common as those of first cousins, and devotional practices as routine as breakfast. Today's readers may feel baffled when they encounter terms such as *Quinquagesima Sunday, particular examen, St. Isaac Jogues, canonical hours.* . . . To help inquisitive readers without cluttering the text with footnotes, we have included an extensive glossary in the back of the book, pages 181-200. There readers will find explanations of virtually all Catholic people and practices mentioned in the book, conveniently arranged in alphabetical order.

LaVonne Neff
Wheaton, IL
February, 1997

Old age can be a holy season, unmarred by the fret of life and the effort to accomplish.

January 13

When Jesus, Who had walked beside His disciples on the way to Emmaus, seemed about to leave them, they urged, "Stay with us, for it is towards evening, and the day is now far spent." And He went in with them. It is towards evening for me. I am very tired, and although I am not yet considered old, I face the fact that old age is not far off, and I beg our Lord to stay with me and let me end in quiet prayer a life that has hitherto been active.

Cardinal Newman, who knew both the trials and joys of age, once wrote that he forever marveled at the old saints, those like St. John the Evangelist and his own St. Philip Neri, who persevered to the end. It is significant that it was the elderly St. John, always mindful of Christ's sympathy for the tempted, who recorded His saying to St. Peter, "But when thou shalt be old, thou shalt stretch forth thy hands, and another shall gird thee and lead thee whither thou wouldst not." If we keep close to our Lord, even if, like Peter, we are crucified, whither we are led is unimportant.

Old age can be a holy season, unmarred by the fret of life and the effort to accomplish; but it has its peculiar temptations. And, whereas much is being written about the increased lifespan, and the words geriatrics and

gerontology—from the Greek word *geron,* an old man—
are familiar to readers of the daily press, we hear little
about spiritual preparation for the years of senescence.

Perhaps I am almost too much aware of the difficulties
that may be ahead of me, for I was constantly with Aunt
Lucy, who lived to be eighty-eight, and with my mother
who reached her eighty-first year, and my volunteer
work in the cancer hospital kept me in the old men's
ward. Watching the elderly, I have concluded that the
holiest among them face reality.

Tonight, beginning this new journal that may last into
my own old age, I find myself saying over and over again
lines from *The Spiritual Canticle* of St. John of the Cross:

> Now I guard no flock nor have I now other
> office. For now my exercise is in loving alone.[1]

And I see, in my mind's eye, my mother, deafened,
somewhat crippled, very frail and weary, sitting in a
rocking chair in her corner, her New Testament and her
rosary beads in her hand. Naturally venturesome, fear-
less, ambitious in her youth, there was no horse too wild
for her, no fence too high; and her intrepidity during her
years of bringing up a family was remarkable; but, once
she became convinced that her active life was at an end,
that her practical means of serving was through prayer,
she prayed. St. John's words remind me of her:

> My soul has employed itself. And all my posses-
> sions in his service:
> Now I guard no flock nor have I now other
> office. For now my exercise is in loving alone.[2]

---

[1] From *The Complete Works of St. John of the Cross,* trans. by
E. Allison Peers (Newman, Westminster, 1949), p. 110.
[2] *Loc. cit.*

*One of the joys of being older is
to see oneself as one of many.*

January 14

On the Feast of the Epiphany, I burned my recent journals. I was not unmindful that they had served as an outlet, but I was thankful to see the pages go up in flames in the fireplace while I sat by the hearth waiting for some neighbors. Glancing through them, I had decided that they preserved not only certain memoranda for *la vie intérieure*, but also records of awkwardnesses that are, I hope, behind me. To write about these was natural: to dwell on them by rereading, to risk the paragraphs' falling into the hands of another, would be unwise. For articulate persons who are so circumstanced that they have little or no intimate conversation, a journal is a safety-valve. This will be different from any previous one, for it will be a notebook for old age, a memorandum in preparation for that union which I hope death will bring, the perfect union with God when at last He dismisses His servant and receives her.

Today I have been thinking of little Cora's asking, when she heard that her maternal grandmother was coming for a visit, "Is she another old lady in black?" I never thought that I would relish the anonymity of being "another old lady in black," but I have discovered that one of the joys of being older is to see oneself as one of many, not singled out by reason of looks or position, but free to sit back unremarked. Somehow, I feel very young when I do this, and almost irresponsible. After all, there is little initiative for me that would not be thought meddling by those of the next generation. And so I can exult in my freedom and in the thought that I am still a child in God's sight, His child.

*Old age, to be holy, must almost necessarily
be a season of contemplation.*

January 15

Two habits are especially important to me now: (1) the practice of the Presence of God, keeping myself, as nearly as possible, mindful of Him and united to Him day and night; (2) the frequent reading of, and meditation on, the Gospels and the Life of our Lord rather than any other books of devotion, because their teachings are the spiritual food on which the contemplative must depend; and old age, to be holy, must almost necessarily be a season of contemplation.

The bearing of these habits is evident. If we live in God's presence, we are exercising our souls in the function that will be theirs throughout eternity, adoration. And, to know the God Whom we adore, we read the Life of Jesus Christ. The time is ahead, perhaps, when it will not be easy to read even the New Testament: when, because of failing eyesight and hearing, we may be without the spiritual books, sermons, much of the help on which we have almost unwittingly relied. Then the familiar Gospels, like the psalms of the Day Hours, will still be at our disposal for meditation.

And, while I can read the Day Hours, I shall continue to do so. None of the geriatrists who have such stress on the importance of schedule in old age, who claim that it furnishes the old with a sense of security to have special occupations at given times, has, insofar as I know, thought to recommend the use of the Day Hours. And what a solace they are! I have leisure to read the psalms and prayers appointed for the day at the canonical hours, and so, alone though I am, I am sharing with hun-

dreds of others the liturgical prayer of the Church. I have
a part in the scheme of things that I am sure any geri-
atrist would approve on the score of mental health. And
David knew life and temptation and cried out for help or
exulted in a way that only the old can truly understand,
so the psalms have a satisfying quality as prayer. The antiphons and the bits of Scripture that make up the Little
Chapters keep memory alive. I love many of the hymns,
especially in the translations that Newman made. None
but Newman, with his constant, haunting sense of passing time, could have rendered so beautifully Prudentius'
hymn for the Lauds of Thursday:

> There is One Who from above
> Watches how the still hours move. . . .

When the still hours have moved on to None, I marvel
at the rightness of his plea, the plea of one who loved
light as no other hymn writer has ever loved it: "Lord,
brighten our declining day."

Of course, the idea of schedule was familiar enough
before either pediatricians or geriatrists emphasized it.
Solomon and St. Augustine, among others, knew the
need. And, for religious, "a rule of life" is considered
essential. For me, my imagination being most readily
captivated by the medieval, Jacopone da Todi's poem
"Of Order" has been a boon. I copied it years ago in
Dante Gabriel Rossetti's translation:

> Set Love in order: thou that lovest Me.
> Never was virtue out of order found;
> And, though I fill thy heart desirously
> By thine own virtue, I must keep my ground.
> When to My love thou dost bring charity

Even she must come with order girt and gown'd.
Look how the trees are bound
To order bearing fruit
  And by one thing compute
  In all things earthly, order's grace and gain.
All things that I had the making of
Were numbered and were measured then by
  Me
And each was ordered to its end by love,
And kept through order, clean for ministry.
Charity, most of all, when known enough
Is of her very nature orderly.
Lo now! What heat in thee
Soul, can have bred this rout?
Thou puttest all order out.
Even this love's heat must be its curb and rein.

I was young when the lines first came to my attention and never dreamed that I would repeat them oftener and oftener when no longer spurred by youth's ardor. But age has its ardor too; its "curb and rein" must be ever at hand.

The lessons against pride which the world gives aid us in finding that rest to the soul that our Lord promises those who learn meekness and humility from Him.

January 16

Of the means to grace, it seems to me none warrants greater attention than the commonest: neglect. (I am not thinking of Mass or the sacraments or prayer, but of the circumstances of our state of life.) All old people are neglected, either physically or otherwise. Their opinions are out of date; their movements are slow; their faculties are impaired (or thought to be). They are cast aside because they impede the swift-running young. Smothered self-esteem, the lessons against pride which the world gives, aid us in finding that rest to the soul that our Lord promises those who learn meekness and humility from Him.

To be forgotten within the family circle—to be, as it were, nonexistent, and yet to be alive—is a very great hardship. So many times, I have watched the hurt expressions on the faces of old people who realized that they were not part of a gathering at which they were present. Yet, I think most of them have the grace to accept their plight inwardly with no resentment, and outwardly with no bitter words, because most have the good sense to recognize the different viewpoints of successive generations.

I realize that no intelligent elderly person can fail to sympathize with modern young people. They have not been conditioned by the reverence inherent in a patriarchal society, and yet, because science, which has not made old people less demanding, has increased the lifespan and made them more numerous, more of the young are called on to serve them than formerly. I gladly school myself to accept youthful intolerance with serenity and dignity, and to meet new ideas cordially, mindful that the ideas of my generation are not invariably right.

Since writing the above lines, I have been smiling to myself over little St. Therese's sense of superiority in the presence of old Sister Peter, whom she voluntarily accompanied from the chapel to the refectory every day. "I had to settle my poor invalid in her place, taking great pains not to hurt her. Then I had to turn back her sleeves, always according to her own rubric, and after this I was allowed to go. But I soon found that she found it very difficult to cut her bread, so I did not leave until I performed this last service. . . . I bestowed on her my sweetest smile."[3] Therese's sweetest smile must have been almost worth being old for, but I can not help but note that the saintly young Carmelite thought age, with its suggestion of end and decay, repellent, and this simple act of charity one to record.

*In my own life, the quiet seasons
have given strength.*

January 17

Yesterday there was a sermon at the mission church on the Gospel of the day, that for the Second Sunday after Epiphany, the wedding feast at Cana. "God gave ten commandments to Moses; Jesus, two to His disciples; but Mary, only one: Whatsoever He shall say to you, do ye." Mary had had Jesus thirty years in His hidden life; it was she who launched Him into His public life. We, His servants, are expected to do simply what He tells us!

Thinking of the hidden life and its length of thirty years in comparison to three of the public, I recalled how often I had marveled at the slowness of unfolding buds, the leisurely "attack" of the finest musicians, the wonderful, quiet precision that goes to the making of all perfection. God, the perfect artist, made all preparation with silent strength. When time was ripe, when, in the eyes of all, Jesus had become mature (He Who had possessed

---

[3] Autobiography (Kenedy, 1926).

infinite wisdom through all ages), then, and then only, was His perfection manifested. Even in my own life, the quiet seasons have given strength. My own present hiddenness may fortify my weak spirit by protecting it from what is most likely to distract. Anyway, the principal thing that our Lord tells me to do is to learn of Him, Who is meek and humble of heart. And Mary tells me to obey.

The practice of the Presence of God becomes increasingly important to me.

January 18

I have been lying on my bed looking at our church steeple silhouetted against the glowing sky. Since so many oak trees fell in the hurricane, I can now see the steeple through the bare branches of those that remain, and beyond it, the lights of the distant city. When I am not well, and can not go to the church to visit the Blessed Sacrament, I derive comfort from this view. I was thinking just now of how, in the beautiful Mass for Corpus Christi that St. Thomas Aquinas composed, the Preface for Christmas is used: ". . . Since by the mystery of the Word made flesh a new ray of Thy glory has appeared to the eye of our souls; that while we behold God visibly, we may be carried by Him to the love of things invisible." The Blessed Sacrament has been, in a special manner, God visible to me, and the very steeple that tops the building that holds the tabernacle serves to remind me of the nearness of the invisible God. The practice of the Presence of God becomes increasingly important to me.

I am not alone, and God will be with me.

January 19

Sometimes I waken in the night as a child is wakened by a nightmare, and, not fully alert at first, come to realize that I am frightened by the thought of lonely old age. Then I recall the Presence of the Holy Spirit. I am not alone, and God will be with me. He will not suffer me to be tempted by the vicissitudes of age above what I am able. St. Paul grew to be old; he was seasoned by suffering when he wrote about temptation. That the years of weary acceptance tempt, there is no shadow of a doubt, and since I know that outward circumstances will not be bettered, the darkness is not lightened by the thought that they might be. I can but trust. In entire abandonment to God's plan for me, I must beg for the faith that will make my soul whole, for, of course, my body is not intended to be.

Just now, I was reading Sext for today, Wednesday. As always, Psalm 56 impressed me: "My heart is ready, O God, my heart is ready: I will sing and give praise." At any time in life, it would be a consolation to have a ready heart, but most, as the days of preparation grow shorter.

Few are improved by sickness.

January 20

My contemporaries would be amused by my preoccupation with the thought of old age and my attempts to make mental provision for its trials. It seems to me a common-sense attitude, and I apply to my consideration of senescence the familiar verses in the *Imitation:*

> Thou mayest do many things whilst thou art
> well; but when thou art sick, I know not
> what thou canst do.
> Few are improved by sickness. . . .

> Keep thyself as a pilgrim and a stranger upon
> earth, to whom the affairs of this world do
> not at all belong.
> Keep thy heart free and raised upwards to God,
> because thou hast here no abiding city.
> Send thither thy daily prayers and sighs with
> tears, that thy spirit may be worthy to pass
> after death happily to the Lord.

Until I wrote that, I had forgotten giving the copy of the *Imitation* that my mother gave me in my girlhood to Mrs. Lee. Like giving my rosary from the Garden of Gethsemane to Mr. Rose, a patient in the cancer ward, it was impulsive, but I have never regretted either. Mrs. Lee read Book III of the *Imitation* as long as she could read, and Mr. Rose was baptized and died a Catholic. The *Imitation* is not for all, perhaps, but there are some young, like the Little Flower, and old, like Aunt Lucy, who find it second only to the Gospels for satisfying spiritual reading.

As we grow older, we are painfully aware of our inadequacy.

January 21

The concert today was beautiful, especially Mendelssohn's Violin Concerto in E Minor, Opus 64, and Beethoven's Fifth Symphony. I found myself thinking there would be violins in Heaven. Perfection of any kind, especially the rendering of a symphony in exquisite harmony, helps me to pray. I never forget that music is of the senses as well as the mind, but, for me, it frees the mind, clears my thoughts, promotes adoration and praise. At the concert, I was asking God's blessings for the musicians, the soloist, the crowd that filled the hall, with a sort of awareness that each individual was God's child. I always do that, now. I do not remember having the habit when I was young, but I suppose that our sympathies widen as we mature, and we realize that a crowd is made up of human beings with joys and sorrows, ambitions and capacities beyond our reckoning.

After the concert, I went to confession. Later, I thought of the difficulty that the old so often have in regard to confession, and especially of Aunt Lucy and her downright refusal to have as her confessor a young priest when she was eighty-five. At the time, it seemed one more incident calling for tact, and I felt that I was humoring her when I made another arrangement for her. Now I know that she was seriously preparing for death, and that she wanted the best help available; an intellectual person, she was not satisfied with the automatic advice to do the best she could. As we grow older, we are painfully aware of our inadequacy, and while others, confessors included, think of our life as behind us, we know that, since we are on the verge of eternity, it is about to begin. Temperamentally unlike Aunt Lucy, I think that I rather prefer a young confessor because he has hope that even a person of my years may improve. After all, with nobody to be tactful for me, I trust the matter to the Holy Spirit and take what I get.

But it has just occurred to me that I have never had a regular confessor of my own generation. When I was young, I found the best direction available that of a much older priest, and now, since his death, I confess to a priest young enough to be my son. In some ways, I suppose, it has been providential, for I was inclined to force myself, and the older priest, knowing the difficult circumstances of my life, was forever urging moderation, thanksgiving, calm, prayer at night rather than crowded into already full days. And now, when I might be tempted to make matters easy for myself, a young confessor, who knows nothing of the wearying years, thinks it best to exact more, and I am convinced that he, too, is right. There is no longer a reason to hoard strength for others' sake, save, of course, sensibly to avoid excessive fatigue or illness that would make me a care; and there is every reason to avail myself of the time left for preparation for Heaven. Taken all in all, a joyous, hopeful young confessor can give a sort of fillip to the dreary efforts of the elderly. I, who naturally say the *De Profundis* at every turn, find myself singing the *Gloria* when going upstairs, that being the prayer of his choosing. Wouldn't he be amazed to know that I still hum the spiritual, "Jacob's Ladder"? I wish I could remember the refrain, "Climb up ye little children, climb up ye olden people, climb to Heaven, climb . . ." or words to that effect. Well, it is time to climb to bed, and it will be the *Gloria* en route.

Tried by life and facing death, [the elderly] need the Holy Eucharist.

January 22

I wonder if there will come a day when there is some special legislation in regard to Holy Communion for those who have passed a certain age. Those who have attained their fifty-ninth year are no longer required to fast in Lent, and I hope that the Church, always taught wisdom by her eminently practical Founder, will take cognizance of the increased lifespan and make it easier for the old to go to Holy Communion. Our Lord instituted the Holy Eucharist immediately before His Passion, thus giving to the apostles, so soon to suffer fear and shame, most intimate communion with Himself as preparation. He knows that the aged are tempted, afflicted, baffled by circumstances, and He gladly fortifies them with His sacramental presence. But, until evening Mass and the possibility of evening Holy Communion become more usual, the weakened elderly will scarcely be frequent communicants unless they are dispensed from the fast. There is a fine independence characteristic of most old people, and a hesitation about asking even a regular confessor for special privilege if they are not ill; "just old age" does not seem to them to be sufficient reason. But, tried by life and facing death, they need the Holy Eucharist.

*To write is to salvage, for I remember best what I
have put into written words.*

January 23

When I wonder if a notebook such as this caters to
introspection, I decide that it does not. In writing out
thoughts that comfort me, and in chronicling little happenings of my life with old people that throw light on
old people's difficulties, I build up a sort of bulwark that
I may need before many years pass. Should God have uses
for me that would let Him trust me to suffer decrepitude
myself, it will help me to bear that state better if I have
stored in memory all relevant aid. When we pause to
look back on any period of life, we see that we had right
to hand all necessary means of grace; not failure in possession but in utilization was the trouble. Young people
scarcely have time to work out for themselves a consis-
tent scheme of action for contingencies, but, as we age,
and remember how often we went into some endeavor
half-equipped, and how nearly worsted we were because
of our lack of preparation, we should be willing to make
ready even for things that may not come to pass. I am
frank enough with myself to admit that it would not be
my own choice to be left here to use for my own needs
the palliatives that I found stood others in good stead, but
I feel that just as our Lord told St. Peter to face matters,
He would tell me. And to write is to salvage, for I
remember best what I have put into written words.

I picked up my old blue notebook in which were jotted
so many entries when I was working twenty-five years
ago on some sketches of the saints. I am humiliated to
see what theoretical knowledge I had of life in the presence of God, and to realize what little use I have made

of what I knew. My paragraphs, reflected as they were from the writings of the saints, seem so infinitely removed from my accomplishment. My reach so far exceeded my grasp, or perhaps I should say exceeded my will and perseverance to attain the perfection pointed out to me, that I can scarcely believe that I penned the lines that I have been reading. Through these I see myself as hopeful, secure in the thought that I was loved and needed. But there was always suffering; and in the records of the effort to bear pain, difficulties, distractions, I recognize the thread of continuity.

I have leisure for the saints again now, and have been given, it seems, *carte blanche* for a prayerful old age, so I am especially interested to note the *motifs* that have persisted through the years: the same thoughts in slightly varied guise have always been comforting; the old tendencies, faults, disinclinations are to a great extent still mine. Meeting myself face to face is humiliating. There is no chance to say that I had not the lesson by heart, for I had, thanks to the New Testament, the *Imitation,* the writings of St. Catherine of Siena, St. Teresa, St. John of the Cross, and St. Francis de Sales. If anything could make me thankful to face age and a fresh start for Heaven, this encounter would. As Catherine of Siena would say, in David's words, "Wait on the Lord, do manfully, and let thy heart take courage: And wait thou on the Lord." Doing manfully ought to be habitual with me, but there are times when being a weak woman is a very appealing role.

*I know old people who are contented because they
have the grace to be so.*

January 24

During a lifetime of watching others' sacrifices, I have
noted many touching rewards. Not in kind, of course, as
a rule, but real rewards, nevertheless. I often think of
how, when Jesus had given sight to the man born blind
"that the works of God might be made manifest in him,"
and the Jews had cast the newly seeing out of the syna-
gogue because he had borne witness to Christ, "Jesus
sought him until He found him." He had let him suffer
the consequences of conversion, but He Himself heard
his profession of faith and comforted him.

Sometimes the world gets a glimpse of the joy of those
who have served God in His little ones. A letter from
Mrs. Mason, this morning. She is eighty now, and I like
to read of her happy old age. She and her husband never
dreamed how they were building for it when, childless
themselves, they befriended her widowed sister's children. Now, a widow, she is a member of a household in
which she is cherished. A maid carries her breakfast to
her, and she spends her days surrounded by nieces and
nephews, and has great-nieces to plan for and knit baby
blankets for.

I have been considering other happy old people of my
acquaintance. Those who live with their own families
and are fortunate enough to be able to serve in some way
are the most contented perhaps; they are more numerous
than they used to be, partly because grandmothers are
willing to do what was formerly left to nursemaids. A
sense of belonging, of helping, of being among their own
is added to their joyful interest in watching the develop-

ment of second and third generations. But I know old people who are contented because they have the grace to be so; some of these have been rejected by their families as troublesome; others have elected to live in nursing homes or boarding houses lest they be a care, or because they cherished their independence. All have worked out a philosophy of accepting their limitations; as the young people would say, "They have adjusted nicely." Not the least happy are those who have means and strength to live alone of their own volition: untrammeled by the routine of family life, they do a little gardening and the homely tasks within their power, think, pray, welcome visitors, maintain a quiet dignity; this manner of life calls for great trust, for faith in one's willingness to change to community living if such becomes desirable; on the whole, it has fewer dangers for mind or body than would be the case were it not for telephones and automatic household devices.

When I ponder the individual problems, I try to remember to pray for those who have hardened their hearts to the old members of their families. It is often necessary for reasons of peace to put the old in boarding places or public homes, but there are instances when it is pure selfishness to do so. I find myself tempted to condemn persons who seem to make no effort to contrive pleasant living conditions for aged relatives, but, always, I recall the fact that I do not know all aspects of the matter, and make allowances for extenuating circumstances with which I am unfamiliar. But, too often, there is a cold deliberation in an arrangement that eventually redounds more to the misery of the young members than the old. The old, seeing themselves cast out, pray with our Lord, "Father, forgive them, for they know not what they do." But the young realize that they do know what they do, and finally are troubled in conscience by the specious reasoning that led to their course.

St. Paul, as practical as the rest of the great mystics, knew the uses of human sympathy.

January 25

I have been reading the Epistle of St. Paul to Philemon and the note on it in the Douay Version. I can not say how many times I have read both before, but not until recently has St. Paul's reference to his own old age impressed me. I like the meager explanation that prefaces the Epistle: "Philemon, a noble citizen of Colossa, had a servant named Onesimus, who robbed him and fled to Rome, where he met St. Paul, who was then a prisoner there for the first time. The apostle took compassion on him and received him with tenderness, and converted him to the faith; for he was a Gentile before. St. Paul sends him back to Philemon with this Epistle in his favour. . . ." After the introductory paragraphs and a few words of praise, St. Paul, with characteristic forthrightness, got down to the matter in hand:

> For charity sake I rather beseech, whereas
> thou art such a one, as Paul, an old man,
> and now a prisoner also of Jesus Christ.
> I beseech thee for my son, whom I have begot-
> ten in my bands, Onesimus,
> Who hath been heretofore unprofitable to thee,
> but now is profitable both to me and thee.

The charming fatherly appeal of the letter is much enhanced by the apostle's reminding Philemon, his disciple, that he is now an old man. So often these days, when reading the communication of my seniors, I am touched by their mentioning their age. St. Paul, as practical as the rest of the great mystics, knew the uses of human sympathy.

Kindness that costs me something in the way of thought and effort seems my best means to atone for the small value I set on the virtue when I was young.

January 26

I believe that even now I could accomplish something if I did not yield to the two weaknesses that prevail with me as with others of my years. I procrastinate; because the days seem shorter than they used to, and my obligations less, I put off writing, calls, small business decisions, finding an excuse for myself in the fact that there is no immediate necessity for me to act, and in the thought that frequently I have been too precipitate.

And I give in to indolence; if there is a question of forcing myself, I fail to do so, especially in matters pertaining to appearances. I give less attention to dress and grooming than I did when others commented on my looks, and I take short-cuts in the house that I thought a servant slovenly for taking. For the first time, I understand all that leads to the slipshod ways of old age. I must be generous enough to make the effort to dress as well as possible for those who must look at me!

Aunt Lucy's mourning in her extreme old age over what she termed her failures used to provoke me. For a person who had accomplished as much as she had, it seemed to me to indicate insincerity on her part, or perhaps, a craving for my denial and praise. I realize that I was to some extent unjust: our failures *do* seem enormous when we look back on them, for it takes great exercise of memory to place them in the mitigating circumstances that our common sense tells us existed. Having lived with a person of Aunt Lucy's temperament, I set myself deliberately to a consideration of what God remembers, and I forget about the shortcomings of my life.

I recall the rush and burden and fatigue incident to life through two world wars, and the most flagrant of my faults seem in part, at least, due to these. But the small meannesses and unkindnesses, the habits of thought and speech that I knew I could and should overcome, are the things for which I try to do penance. Kindness that costs me something in the way of thought and effort seems my best means to atone for the small value I set on the virtue when I was young.

I can not see that an aging Christian has the right to elect a comfortably hazy mental atmosphere.

January 27

Frequently I recall Newman's apparently inspired preparation for old age. He foresaw its temptations and prayed:

"May He support us all the day long, till the shades

lengthen, and the evening comes, and the busy world is hushed, and the fever of life is over, and our work done. Then in His mercy may He give us a safe lodging and a holy rest, and peace at last."

That prayer, so often used in funeral services of the Episcopal Church, is familiar to many who never heard of the Cardinal's poem concerned with dying, *The Dream of Gerontius*. This, written when he was about sixty-eight, close to the time of the brilliant *Apologia,* somehow conveys the peace that the harassed long for. Its serenity and trust appeal to me now as its lyrical beauty did in my girlhood. I repeat to myself the Angel's words to the Soul being carried to Purgatory:

> Softly and gently, dearly ransomed soul,
> In my most loving arms, I now enfold thee,
>
> And, o'er the penal waters, as they roll,
> I poise thee, and lower thee, and hold thee.

No young person, and no old one who had not known the tumult of an agitated, questioning mind, could have written *The Dream of Gerontius*. Nor, of course, Dante's *Purgatorio,* where suffering is assuaged by certainty.

I can not see that an aging Christian has the right to elect a comfortably hazy mental atmosphere. Eternity? Heaven? Purgatory? Hell? Those who have not a clear-cut belief in the tenets of any religion are perhaps unable to face the question of a future life. We modern Christians, who call ourselves practical, are often unwilling to face the thought ourselves. We must die, but why consider death? I imagine the deterrent to be, not a fear of physical passing, for modern medicine has robbed the deathbed of some of its ghastliness, but rather a reluctance to confront a possible weakness in our faith. Death we know to be inevitable. We can do nothing about that. And so we put off the thought of what it leads to, even though we hope that to be the Beatific Vision.

The intelligent make allowances for the limitations of ordinary men and women, but, with their keen minds, they judge Christians' behavior in regard to what is claimed for the Christian way of life.

January 28

Having spent my life largely among Protestants, I am convinced that many of them have faith in the truths dear to us and commend the wisdom of certain rules of the Church. Sometimes we tend to forget that the Gospels and St. Paul's Epistles have been known to them since childhood, and that some of them, in their personal interpretation of the Scriptures, have reached conclusions in accord with Catholic doctrine. The indwelling of the Holy Spirit, so stressed by contemplative orders, is believed in, for instance. I recall that when my father was preparing in middle life for his reception into the Church, the priest instructing him approached the teaching on transubstantiation with some caution, only to be assured, "Yes. I have always believed that." Straight, old-fashioned Protestant training, yet faith in a great essential of Catholic doctrine.

I try to pray for intellectual persons who reach the threshold of faith. In meeting such persons and conversing with them, I know it to be necessary to be careful lest some lack on my part deter any advance on theirs. I do not think that a lack of brilliancy or of articulateness would be as likely to deter as the least failure in charity or kindness. The intelligent make allowances for the limitations of ordinary men and women, but, with their keen minds, they judge Christians' behavior in regard to what is claimed for the Christian way of life: goodness, honesty, love, fortitude, the everyday virtues that Jesus stressed.

The great mystics, with few exceptions, have been in executive positions, or at least doing arduous tasks.

January 29

This feast of St. Francis de Sales has been marked by peaceful thanksgiving for him as my friend. It is curious how we know about some saints and know others. There is that difference for me, say, between St. Francis of Assisi and St. Francis de Sales. I love the former, but I love the latter with a sort of filial devotion such as I would have had had I been his penitent at Annecy. Often his writings have furnished me the answer to something that puzzled, some course in regard to daily living or spiritual direction. When I feel, in a human way, a lack of comprehension in a confessor, I think of St. Francis' assurance that God supplies, that He directs. What it must have meant to gentle people to have Francis, a gentleman by birth and training, as a director! He could feel with them, understand their specific temptations and reactions. His mother and father, both old, were his penitents, and knowing the aged's distress over inability to be recollected, I wonder what he advised. I do not think that, anywhere in his writings, he refers to the difficulty incident to recollection so common in old age. I realize that the great mystics, with few exceptions, have been in executive positions, or at least doing arduous tasks. I suppose that, deep within themselves they have been so attached to God, so united to His will, so nearly identified with Him that, no matter what their preoccupation with mundane things was, they had not the sense of separation that besets me when I become absorbed in my affairs. Doubtless it has been second nature to them to turn to God within their hearts, to let Him teach, direct, counsel.

Suffer the old people to come unto me and forbid them not, for they long for the Kingdom of Heaven.

January 30

An old woman came into the church and knelt near me, clicking her rosary beads and whispering her prayers, "another old lady in black." I found myself paraphrasing our Lord's words, and thinking that He might say, "Suffer the old people to come unto Me and forbid them not, for they long for the Kingdom of Heaven."

Perhaps we take it for granted that we have strong faith until we pass late middle life. Then, we begin to measure our faith by our increasing knowledge of our need of God, and we wonder if we trust, if we even believe, as we might. When I see solitary old men and women kneeling before the tabernacle, I wonder about their prayer. They are God's children, young in His sight. Our Lord does not think them too set in their ways to do better. He increases their hope. For myself, I like to think that in the twinkling of an eye, He can give me the graces that I have implored for decades.

But, at the moment, I feel worsted in regard to Charles and his talent. There is consolation in recalling that hitherto when I thought my efforts wasted and was discouraged, I had no right to be: that, all the time that I was planting and watching and seeing no growth, God was giving the increase without my knowledge. I become more and more aware of the slowness of fructifying, and try to content myself with the tasks of the hour, leaving results to God with truly Pauline trust.

And this reminds me of the words of an old, old saint. Vincent de Paul wrote, in a letter to Mlle. Le Gras: "I try to speak after the manner of the good angels who propose without troubling themselves when their inspirations are unheeded." From one saint to another, for it was St. Louise de Marillac, foundress of the Sisters of Charity, whom he was addressing, the brief statement bears pondering. Recently, I discovered that one of St. Vincent's biographers had applied to him a learned French writer's words: ". . . in as little haste to pass from intention to action as if he had eternity before him . . . the tranquillity of the believer who knows that history is made almost without us. . . ."

With God, we are always children, no matter how old we are.

January 31

Prayer, especially undistracted prayer, does not grow easier as I grow older. The mere mental effort is sometimes exceedingly hard; but the will to pray, trained by long habit, is stronger, and the conviction that prayer is my primary service has been reinforced. I know now, beyond a doubt, that my best means of glorifying God, usually my sole means, is in prayer, whether mental or vocal or the mere acceptance of suffering. The silent, almost imperceptible union of my thought with God's will and my ceding all to Him give the hours meaning. Habitually arid, I offer my distractions, sure that God knows not only that they are not of my choosing, but also that they render me more conscious of my littleness. With God, we are always children, no matter how old we are. And sometimes in dry prayer, I find myself as powerless as a baby, as utterly unable to think as I was in infancy, not even competent to offer a petition save the almost automatic, "God have mercy." And, with the experience of years, I know that there is nothing to do but rest in God's presence as a baby does in its mother's arms. And, after all, rest has its place in the spiritual life.

One night, very tired, kneeling before the tabernacle, I was trying to meditate on our Lord's words, "Learn of Me for I am meek and humble of heart, and you shall find rest to your souls." Usually I had thought of how necessary it was for me to acquire meekness and humility, but that evening, I could think only of the promised rest that would accompany them. Then, our Lord's other words about rest, refreshment, invigoration, began to sing themselves into my memory like a prayerful lullaby. He, Who had no place to lay His head, understood.

I jot down memoranda that pertain rather to a state of soul hoped for than already attained.

February 1

These winter mornings, when I wake before light, I say a rosary for young priests who will have to rouse themselves, touseled and sleepy, to celebrate early Mass. So often, when they stand and say the *Judica me*, they seem scarcely awake, and neither they nor their small servers look as happy as the psalmist suggests they should: "I will go unto the altar of God: to God, Who giveth joy to my youth."

I pray much for young priests. What faith it must take to preach! Even to write down for my own consideration truths that are a part of my daily thought, seems somehow almost hypocritical, for there is so much time when my poor mind is not occupied with the thought of God that I scarcely believe it ever is. "I believe, Lord, help Thou my unbelief" is my plea. To be in the body and concerned altogether with the things of the spirit is, of course, not possible for me; and material things, tangible, commonplace, are easier to write about than spiritual.

But for some of us, to write a thought out is to make it our own in a special way, and, knowing my need to consider my relations with God, not vaguely, but as concretely as possible that they may be more and more important in my mental life, I jot down memoranda that pertain rather to a state of soul hoped for than already attained. When I ponder what I know from reading the Scriptures and the works of the saints, and then examine the actual condition of my soul in the light of that knowledge, I am utterly confounded. A healthy perspective!

Somehow the mystery seems to embody the possibilities that follow on tranquil routine in God's service.

February 2

I love today's feast, the Presentation. Old Simeon, who had so long awaited the coming of Christ, received Him into his arms and said, "Now Thou dost dismiss Thy servant, O Lord, according to Thy word in peace." And eighty-four-year-old Anna, who served in the Temple day and night, was rewarded by the sight of her Savior. It is but recently that I have come to think of the age of the two who greeted our Lady and St. Joseph at the Beautiful Gate, but now I like to consider this aspect of the mystery.

Small wonder the scene appealed to artists as different as Fra Angelico and Rembrandt. I have never forgotten the face of Simeon in Fra Angelico's fresco in San Marco in Florence; surely its expression is one of the loveliest ever portrayed. Lately, I happened upon Rembrandt's etching, "The Presentation in the Temple in the dark manner," dated 1654, and hung in the Metropolitan Museum in New York. A commentator has written of it, "With the eyes of his spirit the old man sees a glory that

Rembrandt shows us with the richest, most flashing black-and-white ever etched." Indeed, the effect of light and shadow is such that one almost inevitably exclaims, "A light to the revelation of the gentiles, and the glory of Thy people Israel"! It seems to me that Rembrandt, so felicitous in depicting the aged, was never more so than in this work. Simeon's rapture indicates that the promise of the Holy Ghost had been fulfilled: ". . . that he should not see death before he had seen the Christ of the Lord."

I took down the *Divine Comedy* just now, for I thought that I recalled that Dante had described an intaglio of the Presentation along with the exquisite one of the Annunciation in Canto X of the *Purgatorio*. But he did not. And now I remember that it is in another poem of mystical love, one written by St. John of the Cross, that Simeon figures:

> Till he saw the ever living
> God descending from above
> Took Him in his arms and held Him
> And embraced Him in his love.

Somehow the mystery seems to embody the possibilities that follow on tranquil routine in God's service. Simeon in the round of his duties was in the Temple, as was Anna, whose calling kept her there. And Mary and Joseph, poor and unquestioning, offering a pair of turtle doves, were but following the law of their fathers when they were told, ". . . this Child is set for the fall and for the resurrection of many in Israel. . . ."

Where speech would avail nothing, there is
wisdom in a passive attitude to others.

February 3

I believe that the old deceive themselves very little:
perhaps because they have made futile attempts to do so
for so long. And, in like manner, they are seldom
deceived by others: long experience has given them an
ability to estimate character, to note when persons put a
false value on things, give mere lip-service, are insincere,
perhaps unintentionally. There are occasions when the
old have the duty to speak plainly; they can do so without personal condemnation, but with ethical perception
due to recognition of right and wrong. Certain hard
truths are most readily accepted by the intelligent when
stated by a sensible old man or woman, and the aged
have nothing to lose in a worldly way, and much to gain
in a spiritual, by complete mental and social honesty.
But, where speech would avail nothing, there is wisdom
in a passive attitude to others. I treasure the right to reticence in such cases. Youth would lose much of its charm
were it not ingenuous and outspoken, and reticence in
the young is sometimes a fault; but it becomes a virtue in
the old, who are so often tempted to garrulousness. For
myself, I admit that I derive great peace from the thought
that relief from a lifelong burden of responsibility for
others is part of my liberty as a child of God nearing
Heaven.

Remorse is a state of mind best known to little children . . . and to old people.

February 4

Maybe remorse is a state of mind best known to little children in the simplicity of their sorrow over wrong-doing, and to old people. In middle age, life pushes and crowds; contrition, no matter how sincere, is not to be lingered over and indulged in, but must incite to reparation through good works. I used to watch an elderly man, whose youth had not been exemplary, in the church. He would make the Stations devoutly. Then he would kneel before the altar for a fresh Act of Contrition, and begin again the Way of the Cross. A simple man, he was sorry, and following the Man of Sorrows. I like to think that our Lord reminded him that when he was giving scandal in his early life, he did not reckon the magnitude of his offenses. After all, it is a comfort to remember in one's last years that our Lord could beg pardon for most on the score that, not knowing Him well, ". . . they know not what they do."

Jesus, Whose delight is to be with the children of men, doubtless has great joy in the visits of those who have been His through long years.

February 6

I asked a very old and holy confessor what one must do to be holy in old age. "What do you expect to do throughout eternity?" he inquired. "To adore God, I hope." "Begin now," he counselled, and added, "and be like a little child."

I think of that when I see some elderly persons. Going into the chapel at the Home the other day, I noted a frail, blue-eyed old lady wrapped in a pretty light blue shawl. Her wheel-chair was drawn up behind the Sisters who were reciting the office. She did not seem to be engaged in any special form of prayer herself. I recalled little Aunt Lucy, who used to say, after she grew old, that she sat before the Blessed Sacrament telling our Lord not only that she loved Him, but also that she knew that He loved her. Perhaps some such thoughts were in this old lady's mind. Jesus, Whose delight is to be with the children of men, doubtless has great joy in the visits of those who have been His through long years. Were I perfectly recollected in church, I would not observe the aged adorers as I do. But, just as I watch the antics of the school-children and altar boys and smile with our Lord, asking Him to make saints of the culprits, so I ask help for His old, old friends who totter in to tell Him of their love.

I am receiving so much from God's bounty. All that I can do is to marvel and to thank Him.

February 7

When I drove into the driveway this evening at seven, I paused to look through the bare oak trees for the lights of the city, for it has been one of those crystal days when the buildings were in clear view. Just as I had anticipated, the skyscrapers were aglow in the distance, but I had forgotten that the moon would be rising, and was startled to see how large it was and how near it seemed as it came up. It is wonderful to live in the oak woods and yet have a vista of one of the most thickly settled areas in the world. When I see the brilliant lights, ruby, emerald, topaz, and am entranced by the loveliness, and puzzled that one as unworthy as I should have the joy of such a scene, I think of our Lord's parable in last Sunday's Gospel, and the generosity of the householder who said, ". . . is it not lawful for me to do what I will?" Like those who came last and were paid, I am receiving so much from God's bounty. All that I can do is to marvel and to thank Him.

For a Christian, there is no such thing as inactivity.

February 8

I think that the fact that I have no need to choose conduces to serenity. I remarked once in a sermon of St. Bernard's: "Even a holy man feels grave uncertainty between the claims of fruitful labor and of restful contemplation; and, although he is always occupied about good things, yet he always feels a sense of regret as if he had been doing that which is wrong, and from one moment to another entreats with groans to be shown the will of God. In these uncertainties the one and only remedy is prayer and frequent uplifting of the soul to God that He would deign to make continually known to us what we ought to do, and when, and in what manner we should do it." And I have always cherished the story of St. Philip Neri's sending one of his disciples to put a hospi-

tal apron on another, who was praying before the
Blessed Sacrament, with the message that it was time to
leave Christ for Christ. If I were younger and physically
stronger, I might wonder about my course. As it is, I,
who would not have had the wisdom to choose the best
part, have had it allotted to me.

After an active life, I find it hard to waken to the
thought of an inactive day. But, for a Christian, there is
no such thing as inactivity. My very abandonment to
God's will, my acquiescence to my nothingness in the
scheme of things, partake of service if rightly understood, for such union with His will, such surrender to
Him, become prayer. Even if I do not make as much use
of my enforced leisure as I might for mental or vocal
prayer, the acceptance of it as God-given is pleasing to
God as an offering of my will.

It is hard to bear spiritual dryness in late life.

February 9

It is hard to bear spiritual dryness in late life, for it
seems part of our general condition: we are weary of
ourselves, and we provoke in others nothing of the glad
response with which youth meets: we have no sensible
consolation in anything. But, if we have tried up to now,
our will to love has developed through the years. We will
to pray: will to love: . . . and trust!

I wonder how many pray consistently for the old;
probably few save the nuns who devote their lives to
serving them in homes and hospitals. When I look out at
the lights of neighboring communities at night, and then

to the glow of the city in the distance, I try to ask God's help for the old in hospitals, especially those with chronic illness, and above all, for cancer patients whose malady is such a trial for themselves and their families. Chronic sickness, whether in the old or young, is soon accepted by those who surround the sufferers; the novelty of the situation wears off: the patients must adapt themselves to being set apart for pain without being catered to as invalids; willy-nilly, they are cast for a role of heroism. The aged and the chronic sick have a special right to my prayer.

We are in fairy land this morning.

February 10

We are in fairy land this morning. Every branch and twig of every tree and shrub is lightly decked in soft white snow. The black oaks seem to be laughing to themselves, pretending that they are garlanded in blossoms, but the more fragile trees and bushes bend in gracious acceptance; they are not overladen as they would be were they coated in ice, merely weighted enough to bow serenely to the white earth. The sky is blue, the sun shines, and there is a grey squirrel in the grey beech tree by my window.

God asks tremendous courage of the aged.

February 11

The feast of our Lady of Lourdes. "I am the Immaculate Conception," said the Lady to Bernadette in the child's own patois. Later, when Bernadette told of the happening, she insisted that, had there been a more ignorant child in the countryside, our Lady would have chosen that child to hear her revelation. The sinlessness of Mary and the innocence of the little saint are entirely spiritual in quality, yet it is of the healing of the body that most persons think when Lourdes is mentioned.

That freedom from sin and bodily healing have been linked at Mary's shrine is no wonder. Our Lord was quick to say, when He worked a miracle, "Thy sins are forgiven thee." And, when He gave sight to the man born blind, He replied in answer to His interrogators, "Neither hath this man sinned nor his parents, but that the works of God might be made manifest in him."

To me, Lourdes, in the summer, when the national pilgrimage trains arrive laden with the very ill, and the town swarms with stretcher bearers and other volunteers, seems a place apart: the grace of its miracles no greater than the grace of acceptance accorded those not cured.

We of the twentieth Century have been so influenced by the advances in the scientific care of the body, by the wonders wrought by modern surgery and drugs, that our whole attitude to physical suffering in ourselves or others is one of hope for cure. This is doubtless the right approach. Yet, if we bend all our energy toward cure, and tend to forget the uses of pain, we may be weakening our power to bear the unavoidable. The aged who sensibly face the fact that pain is theirs for the rest of their lives, that wearisome effort to cure is worse than the affliction, can school themselves to offer pain in glad atonement, undistracted by any thought of how to rid themselves of it.

God asks tremendous courage of the aged. Often theirs is a slow martyrdom; minute by minute they are called on to suffer an increase of physical pain and mental loneliness, and to realize more acutely as the hours pass that, in this life, assuagement is unlikely. But they have experiential knowledge of God's mercy, and the belief that God will give for each new test, actual grace.

Newman, who lived so much in his own mind, wrote in his poem *Semita Justorum:*

> . . . trial did convey,
> Or grief, or pain, or strange eventful day,
> To my tormented soul such larger grace.

He wrote next of the "shadow of the Providential Hand." He was young when he wrote those lines, and I was young when they first impressed me. But neither of us was a stranger to suffering.

It always seems to me that a child's attitude to sickness is the only sensible one for the old. It is practical in the extreme. A child does not complicate illness by the thought of better or worse; when he is better, he forgets the past; when he is worse, he is ready to be diverted if possible. There is for him no question of suffering at the thought of his own suffering that Pascal prayed to be spared, and that the unbelieving endure. When I find myself worn and weary and ill, I must beg God to teach me not to aggravate matters by being troubled by my condition.

The ability to avoid worry over my woes grows as I become more and more aware that their season is limited:

> Let nothing disturb thee;
> Let nothing affright thee.
> All things are passing.
> God only is changeless.
> Patience gains all things.
> Who hath God wanteth nothing.
> God alone sufficeth.

From my girlhood, I took comfort in those lines of St. Teresa's, and especially in "All things are passing." I had not her vivid sense of God's presence, of course, but the conviction that hard things did not last forever was strong in me. When I was ill for so long, that line and several in Sidney Lanier's *The Marshes of Glynn* would run through my head in the iterate fashion that fever promotes. I must have said them aloud sometimes, for, now and then, for years afterwards, my mother would note my expression and murmur allusively, "All things are passing," or ". . . good out of infinite pain." In age, it is still a comfort to lean on St. Teresa's common sense, the common sense of a mystic, and so distilled to the ultimate. Not being a St. Paul, I can not claim to glory in my infirmities. But I do feel that certain graces have come in sickness and perhaps because of sickness, and that pain has had a modifying influence. There is a training here that is not of choice, but which gives confidence, nevertheless.

He suffered for us because He wanted to.

February 12

A little girl has been coming into the church when I am making my visit. Today, I called her to me and asked her why she was not at play with the children outside. She explained, "You see, I had a little bit of polio." Then, looking at the crucifix, she asked me if I knew about Jesus, and informed me, "He suffered for us because He wanted to."

What [God] wants is humility, a true estimate of ourselves in relation to Himself.

February 13

The church was crowded this morning, and there was so much confusion that I was trembling and almost in tears by the time I reached the communion rail. The child who had had "a little bit of polio" came and knelt near me. She was serene as she waited for our Lord Who "wanted to suffer for us." I tried to be at least willing to suffer.

Being so crowded in our parish church somehow offends my dignity, as it should not, of course, for, save in God's sight, I am little and nothing. I have a soul created by God for His glory, and that is precious to Him and to me . . . but to all the millions and millions who have lived, are living, will live in this world which is in itself an infinitesimal speck in the universe! It would not be wise to impress the thought of unimportance too much on a young person, lest there be too little effort on his or her part. However, the individual has an urge, a God-given *ego,* that pushes. When the push is directed, as in a St. Paul (who, according to my mother, was a great egotist) or a St. Teresa, the *ego* knows itself as God's and measures its littleness by what it can imagine of God's greatness. What St. Paul and St. Teresa recognized early, it is given to lesser beings to understand late; too late, in a human way, perhaps, but not too late in God's providence, for what He wants is humility, a true estimate of ourselves in relation to Himself. If our endowment is ordinary, we are seldom intelligent enough to see this clearly in early life; therefore, to see it in old age is a grace.

I speak too seldom of God.

February 14

I know that I speak too seldom of God because I have lived among worldly people and have been conventional in utterance, but now that I am older, and lacking in the self-consciousness and timidity of youth, I do speak in such a matter-of-fact way that sometimes it startles even myself. I remember noting this in my mother. It seemed almost as if, nearing Heaven, the thought of God and God's teaching came unbidden, and was mentioned unremarked by herself. No uneasiness ever resulted. Others had been thinking what she put into words, and so were not shocked by what might have seemed a want of reticence.

Because I have nothing of my own,
the emptiness is full of God.

February 15

Lately, things have seemed to go awry, and I have been trying to console myself with the fact that all of my fruitless efforts and my own futility have their uses in the Divine Economy. God has used my previous failures. I must abandon all to His will, not in cowardly surrender, but with willingness to try again. If He empties me of all self-esteem, I will be worth more.

Poor Francis Thompson! None will ever know what he had suffered of weakness and disgrace before he wrote, ". . . must Thou char the wood ere Thou canst limn with it?"

Depression is for me who am naturally buoyant, almost invariably ascribable to physical malady. Recently, I have felt like one imploring help in a cold, black silence, one whose every move was thwarted, who felt millions of miles away from those present. There has been no sweetness in prayer, a terrible dryness. Yet, there has been the comfort of knowing that now my prayer is solely for God's sake: because He wills my effort. So, in a way, the vast waste is satisfying: because I have nothing of my own, the emptiness is full of God. I have no sensation of pleasure, but a peace so sterile that it seems part of my general numbness. I can but offer God this blankness, as I would offer Him physical pain.

When I was a child, I used to go with Aunt Lucy to the Lenten sermons in the church of San Silvestro in Capite in Rome. Great English preachers were chosen to deliver these sermons, and, in after years, I was interested to hear Aunt Lucy naming the speakers whom we had heard. Nothing has remained to me of any of the discourses save one illustration. In a slum district school, in one of the British manufacturing cities, Manchester or Birmingham, perhaps, the children were having physical examinations. One little girl came back to the classroom from the doctor's office, and the Sister in charge asked, "Monica, what did the doctor say about you?" "He said," the child replied, "that I was a poor miserable specimen of humanity." Then, pirouetting merrily, she added, "But *he* didn't know that I had made my First Communion." This has been one of the days when I have kept reminding myself that I have made my First Communion!

How I do delight in the gusto of initial success!

February 17

In the mail, a letter from Esther to tell me of the acceptance of a manuscript. It is a joyful letter, full of excitement, the kind of communication that gives me untold pleasure. I feel touched when young writers share their enthusiasm with me. When I am pressed for time, and wish that I could be spared the reading of stories or verses or articles, even book-length manuscripts, I remember these letters that come occasionally. The novelty of publication wears off when those whose first efforts were presented for my approval have a wider public than just me, and they and I are likely to forget the first effervescence, the editor's letter, the small check, the marked copy (printed in letters of gold)! But how I do delight in the gusto of initial success! After reading this letter, I thought of Fred's excitement when telling me on the telephone of the arrival of his first payment from a publisher; suddenly, the thrilling voice at the other end of the line was gone, and only the sounds of a tussle came over the wire, then the agonized wail, "The puppy got hold of my check!"

There are no more explicit promises in the Gospels than those that relate to the indwelling of the Holy Spirit.

February 18

It is not necessary to raise my heart in prayer, just to open it to God present.

The young pray like novices in any undertaking, more conscious of their relationship to the work than of the work itself. One of the joys of prayer in later life is its being second nature. After long years, the awkwardness of the apprentice is forgotten, and the soul plunges headlong into communion with God.

Certainly, for the lonely old, there is no happier practice than that of the Presence of God. If I realize that I am lonely merely because I forget that I am not alone, I am straightway aware of watchful, interested, loving companionship. There are no more explicit promises in the Gospels than those that relate to the indwelling of the Holy Spirit.

A little later, I shall push aside some mulch and peep at the bulb beds.

February 19

   As I drove home from Mass this morning, I could see a promise of spring. Across the blue sky, there floated just a suggestion of stratus, and in the sunlight, a timid green showed on the lawns; the bare branches of the maple trees have become a purplish-grey, and the rhododendron leaves are broad, no longer the tightly curled fingers of an old Doré illustration. We have not yet said good-bye to winter, but, a little later, I shall push aside some mulch and peep at the bulb beds. It is wonderful to me that the very frailest of the flowers are the first to dare the elements; they have not long to sport their bloom and prefer to do so before the sun is too strong. There are green leaf buds on my lilac bush that I have been nursing since it came up as a shoot. The parent bush, a double white lilac, always bloomed twice a year, in May and October. I picked white lilacs as well as white chrysanthemums in the garden on an autumn day. I am anxious to see if the young lilac is as ambitious!

One of the best habits [Cardinal Gibbons] taught me was to close my eyes.

February 20

   The church was crowded this morning and I thought of my mother. I formerly ascribed to her deafness her horror of confusion, but I note that the tendency to avoid tumult is common in the elderly. Perhaps the nerve strain of a lifetime is cumulative, and outward agitation exhausts proportionately. Then, throughout life, there has been a subconscious anticipation of peace: confusion disappoints that. I seek a quiet place in church or a protected seat on a train or ship much as my mother did, not for lack of interest in what is happening nearby, but to shelter myself from physical fatigue. And, if I must be in the midst of confusion? I shut my eyes. When I was a girl, I used to watch Cardinal Gibbons, already an old man, sitting in a church or auditorium with his eyes closed. I soon learned that he was not taking the nap that others might suppose, for there was never an occasion when he did not rise and allude pertinently to the words of a previous speaker. He was saving his nerves and energy by dropping his lids. I laugh when I realize that one of the best habits he taught me was to close my eyes.

I can thoroughly understand why Mother and Aunt Lucy . . . were exasperated with . . . Cicero.

February 21

I remember a group before the statue "*Una Vecchia*" in the Capitoline Museum. An elderly person was fascinated by the pitiless portrayal of a crone, while the middle-aged moved away in horror. A truly ebullient and very young classicist had no qualms. "Read *De Senectute*," he advised. "A wonderful book! Cicero could enjoy old age."

I sat down just now and read *De Senectute* with an eye to an old person's judgment of it. I can thoroughly understand why Mother and Aunt Lucy, on whom Tom was constantly pressing it in the last years of their lives, were exasperated with him and with Cicero. What Cicero, a man of words, of well-arranged and convincing platitudes, wrote of the joys of age did not entertain them. Two old people, who had spent their childhood in a country ravaged by war and so-called "Reconstruction," had then endured the trials of two world wars, and lost in one their dearest, were not comforted by Cicero's smooth phrases. "There is, however, a calm and serene old age which belongs to a life passed peacefully, purely and gracefully, such as we learn was the old age of Plato, who died while writing in his eighty-first year." That mattered little to the aged in my family, nor were they as much impressed by the fact that Sophocles wrote a play at ninety as was the orator.

As I grow older, I try to train myself to expect no recognition save God's.

February 22

As I grow older, I try to train myself to expect no recognition save God's. He knows. He sees. Humanly, I want expressed gratitude when I have spent time, money, strength for others' pleasure. Perhaps that is because I lack the simplicity to do everything entirely for God. I try to have blind faith in others' motives, feeling that, were they fully aware, they would be more generously responsive. My mother, in her old age, was conscious of the inarticulateness of those to whom she gave lavishly; yet, she did not let seeming ingratitude deter her.

It is God's will for a Christian to know Him through Christ.

February 23

I have been reading the 14th, 15th and 16th chapters of St. John's Gospel, for, in dryness, no spiritual reading helps me as much. There are times when the psalms answer, and times when I can get comfort in reading the Epistles to the Romans, Colossians, Ephesians, and Philippians, or St. John's charming letters urging us to love one another; but, when aridity reaches its maximum, as it has today, nothing serves but our Lord's consoling words recorded by His Beloved Disciple. Read slowly, pondered, even if we have had them by heart for years, these chapters spur to a new knowledge of our relationship with Jesus. I used to wonder if there were something very wrong with me that all my love of God was enfolded, so to speak, in my love of Jesus. And now that I am older, I know that it is God's will for a Christian to know Him through Christ. Indeed, I know so little of the Godhead, that there is no marvel that I cling like a dry burr to our Lord's mantle.

It is, I think, beyond the power of the average child or man to put doctrine into original words.

February 24

I am thankful for everything that I know by heart, and especially for the New Testament passages. As school girls, we memorized the Sunday Gospels word for word. How little any of us, standing to repeat them in the old study hall, knew the comfort they would bring us! When the advisability of having children memorize what they do not understand is questioned, I recall how our Lord's words that I did not fully understand, perhaps, remained in my mind for consolation and enlightenment when I was mature enough to meditate on them. As for the *Baltimore Catechism*, with its questions and answers so far beyond the grasp of the child who knows it word for word, it has been a bulwark to me all through my life. "What does your Church teach about this or that?" a Protestant will ask me, and, thinking perhaps of my father in his armchair hearing us repeat our catechism lesson, I answer exactly what I was taught to answer in words so simple and correct that I have no need to expatiate on Catholic doctrine. "That is what my Church teaches," I can assure the interrogator. But when I was stumbling over the lesson, and had the catechism returned to me time and again with the admonition to get each phrase in sequence, I did not understand what I memorized. It is, I think, beyond the power of the average child or man to put doctrine into original words: the theologian might do so, but even he would find it difficult to employ a terminology comprehensible to the questioner.

I am certain that, as we age, we must trust our own judgment in dealing with our limitations.

February 25

I am learning a measure of caution that St. Paul might not approve, for he believed in the effort to be all things to all men. For so long I spent myself to the utmost for any human being. Doing so I found that, all too often, whereas the sacrifice was beneficial to me at the time, the mere fact that I could not make a continuous feat of it led to some estrangement. So I shall try for moderation in all things, also a Pauline ambition. I am certain that, as we age, we must trust our own judgment in dealing with our limitations. I have not the strength that I once had, and I am sure that there are situations in which my normal supply of patience would be quickly exhausted. Of late, I deliberately avoid being pressed into endeavor to which I am unequal. I create for myself a little Egypt, purely imaginary, but a refuge when I am harassed by the overactive.

All that I can ask is, "Jesus, Son of David, have mercy on me."

February 27

This is Quinquagesima Sunday, and I am looking toward Lent. Even last year, I could pray with the blind man in today's Gospel, "Lord, that I may see." Now, all that I can ask is, "Jesus, Son of David, have mercy on me." What the man saw first, when Christ gave him sight, was the Son of Man on His way to Jerusalem to suffer.

[God] does not ask labored meditation or unlabored ecstasy.

March 1

My prayer is so often a dumb prayer, simply stupid stillness, no mental activity, or, if there is any, a series of silly distractions. Yet, it is serene, for I am entirely dependent on God, and now know that I am. He does not ask labored meditation or unlabored ecstasy, what He asks is my *fiat*, my union of my will with His. This prayer is marked by willing, peaceful surrender to God's choice.

It is the prayer of the old. It asks no delight, no enlightenment. Were it not wordless, it would be expressed in the words of Christ: "Father, into Thy hands I commend my spirit."

I am reminded by others' behavior that I am unimportant.

March 2

At Mass this morning, Ash Wednesday, I prayed especially to be in entire accord with the Church throughout Lent. It is significant that the Church points out now the necessity of complete spiritual honesty. We are warned to lay aside all pretense: to be, rather than to seem, good. We are to be concerned not with what others think we are, but with what we are in fact.

It might be supposed that those passing middle-age would not be vain: they know that they look old and that they are not robust. But poor human nature cries out in them for recognition: perhaps they like to tell what they have accomplished or what possessions they have had: perhaps they want to be thought independent, self-sufficient, no care to others. This temptation to vanity and lack of sincerity is insidious. While I have full use of my faculties, I am determined to train myself to the thought that it does not matter what I am, save in God's sight. This is not too hard, for I am reminded by others' behavior that I am unimportant. But I must make a positive effort to be my plain self and "to abide under the protection of the God of Heaven." The Church employs the psalm from which that is taken, Psalm 90 in the Douay Version, in the Lenten liturgy, and I am glad, for so many of its verses are pertinent that it is the old people's psalm.

As for carrying my cross bravely through Lent, as preachers advise: years ago I discovered that my disposition was part of my cross, and bearing with myself, a burden not of my choosing. I would have wished to be patient, placid, tractable instead of quick-on-the trigger, outspoken, intolerant.

[Mary] was thoroughly in sympathy with our Lord's sacrifice of Himself.

March 4

I have been considering when making the Stations of the Cross and reciting the Sorrowful Mysteries of the Rosary, our Lady's perfect willingness that our Lord should suffer because her will was entirely united with His. She accepted the pain that was vicarious along with her actual personal sorrow, but, beyond this, she was thoroughly in sympathy with our Lord's sacrifice of Himself.

The happiness of a heart overflowing with generosity is evident.

March 5

At the beginning of Lent, I think of the joy that pervades the Gospel accounts of our Lord's prophecies of the Atonement. There is more than a hint of gladness in His introduction of the thought of the Passion. The grain of wheat falls into the ground and dies that it may bring forth fruit: the Son of Man must be lifted up that He may draw all to Himself. The happiness of a heart overflowing with generosity is evident. The act of redemption was the supreme act, and the day was close at hand.

But, joyful in His own right, Jesus knew that pain was in store for His disciples. Like a good physician, He prepared their minds that they might suffer with least shock to themselves. As we age, we better appreciate the prevenience of Jesus. He teaches us to face the future in a matter-of-fact way.

[Jesus] gives the Bread of Heaven to those who ask.

March 6

The church was crowded again this morning, and as the parishioners thronged at the communion rail, I thought of how Jesus was pressed by the multitude in Palestine. Here, as there, He knows each individual as His. He gives the Bread of Heaven to those who ask. While I waited my turn, I tried to unite myself in spirit with the humanity that He loves, and offer Him not only my poor little self but all mankind.

Nothing prevents constant thanksgiving for the lifelong privilege [of daily Holy Communion].

March 7

This is the feast of St. Thomas Aquinas, for me the saint of the Blessed Sacrament rather than the author of the *Summa*. My generation was one of the first to benefit by Pope Pius X's decree on Frequent Communion. We have grown old dependent on the Holy Eucharist. It is a very real hardship for those accustomed to daily Holy Communion to be so handicapped that they must await others' pleasure to get to Mass or to receive the sacraments at home. But nothing prevents constant thanksgiving for the lifelong privilege. And Spiritual Communion, a habit dear to our Jansenist-ridden forebears, is any moment ours.

Just to know that there are Little Sisters who welcome the pitiful old who have nobody else, warms my heart.

March 8

Two Little Sisters of the Poor called this morning. When I see their black wagon draw up before the door, and the two, with their ample black mantles and tiny white face-ruffs descend, I know that I am in for a merry half-hour. Their old driver evidently does, too, for he settles down for a comfortable rest outside. They have to tell me about Bonne Mère and the Little Family. All members of the Little Family are supposed to be over sixty and without resources, but they are men and women of any race or creed. I inquire about any whom I know, and they tell me about others and about an author whose stories I enjoyed when I was young, now one of their charges. Then we drift into French and discuss Biarritz and Paris and other places where Sister Anne has served; and her companion rises and wanders around the room, noting especially the lucinas that remind her of those in her childhood home abroad. Sometimes they hand me a picture of Sister Mary of the Cross, who, as Jeanne Dugan, a great-hearted woman of Brittany, took into her home and nursed a penniless old woman. Other working women joined her, other old people were cared for, and finally the order of the Little Sisters of the Poor came into being. My Sisters belong to one of the hundreds of homes which, since 1840, have sprung up all over the world, and it seems to me that they are as simple as Jeanne Jugan was. I like to recall that she, really the foundress, lived as an ordinary member of the Community in France, her history being unknown to some of the novices in her institution. After we have chatted awhile, I hand my offering to Sister Anne. She puts it into her great pocket without looking at it, but gives me many a sweet God Bless You. Sometimes there are clothes here, a warm coat or a bit of finery (old people love pretty things), or some dishes; then the wagon is requisitioned. One day, I said, "Sister, I am coming to you." "Why not?" she demanded. "You have had your training." "Oh, not as a Sister," I demurred, "coming to live with you." I had heard that the Sisters ate what the patients declined, if there were anything, and . . . well, maybe had I had a religious vocation, that would have given me pause in my choice of an order. But just to know that there are Little Sisters who welcome the pitiful old who have nobody else, warms my heart. And who knows but that they will eventually shelter me with their Little Family? They like to give their old people small tasks about the Home. Maybe they could use my green thumbs in the garden if I am not too stiff to stoop by then. I prefer digging to darning, but thanks to long practice, I am no tyro at mending the heel of a sock, and there are plenty of socks. I can never pass a Little Sister stationed at the door of a city shop, or making her rounds of the markets with her basket, without pausing for her God Bless You. My offerings are not scrutinized, but are acknowledged with a Little Sister smile.

*The average woman who has kept house has
had a multitude of trivial duties and trials that,
unless she was very superior, distracted from
contemplative prayer.*

March 9

A season of freedom from exhausting duty, a season
for prayer, is welcome enough to some women in old
age. The average woman who has kept house has had
a multitude of trivial duties and trials that, unless she
was very superior, distracted from contemplative prayer;
indeed, if conscientious, in an effort to fulfill well the
offices thrust upon her, she is likely to have become
exacting, a domestic perfectionist. And the interruptions
that beset a housekeeper! I often wish that my Guardian
Angel were as accommodating as he who had charge of
St. Frances of Rome, and would mark my place for me
in gold when I am interrupted when reading my prayers.
If I were as much given to prayer as St. Frances? Well, anyway, this is her feastday, and I was thinking of the bright
camellias that adorned her house in Rome years ago. They
made a much greater impression on my childish mind
than either prayer or angels.

*Whatsoever I have or hold, Thou hast given it,
I give it all back to Thee and commit it wholly
to be governed by Thy will.*

March 10

A Jesuit with a youthful face gave a brief talk on surrender after Mass this morning. There were very few in the
church, and later, seeing him kneeling there, I wondered
whether to tell him that I thought the talk would have
pleased St. Ignatius Loyola, so much was it the embodi-
ment of his prayer, the well-known *Suscipe:*

> Receive, O Lord, all my liberty. Take my
> memory, my understanding and my entire
> will. Whatsoever I have or hold, Thou hast
> given it, I give it all back to Thee and commit
> it wholly to be governed by Thy will. Thy love
> and thy grace give unto me, and I am rich
> enough and ask for nothing more.

Having decided that at my age nobody could misun-
derstand my speaking, I did, and his smile of gratitude
for my expression touched me. He had not thought to
mention the prayer, so he must have been pleased to
realize how he had absorbed its teaching.

I have loved that *Suscipe,* and now, when I feel particularly barren of everything, I remember how many
times I have uttered it, and reproach myself that I am not
happier at the thought of having been taken at my word.

*Aloneness, after a full life, may be rich
in peace and joy.*

March 11

Doubtless one of the greatest assets for a happy old age is the ability to enjoy being alone. Solitude is frequently the lot of the elderly, and those who can love it rather than be irked by it are fortunate. It seems to me that there is a great difference between what we dub loneliness and aloneness . . . the former having a connotation of sadness, the latter being rather negative. Loneliness begets many temptations. Aloneness, after a full life, may be rich in peace and joy. Just as one may be lonely without being alone, so one may be alone without being lonely.

One must be practical to be holy.

March 12

The literalness of the saints, their common sense in God's service, appeal to me: there is nothing vague and romantic about sanctity; one must be practical to be holy. I have been thinking about the fact that St. Gregory the Great did penance when he learned that a man had died of starvation in Rome when he was Pope. That seems to me an entirely logical action; Rome was his city, his responsibility, and he felt it incumbent on him to see that no citizen starved.

*I believe in my heart that most
people are truly kind.*

March 13

Because of the rapidity of communication, no other
generation ever has been as quickly informed of world-
wide happenings as ours. For the sensitive, this is in a
way part of the individual's share in the sufferings of
mankind. To be forever aware of disasters in remote
corners of the earth, to hear of war, crime, floods,
famine, exhausts the sympathetic. Wickedness is so
much more stressed in our press than goodness that it is
necessary to make conscious effort to recall the generosity elicited by catastrophe, and the inherent kindness of
most of the millions of human beings in the world. I
believe in my heart that most people are truly kind. The
apathy developed in metropolitan districts is a protective
one; it is scarcely possible to endure association without
it; were the sympathies given full sway, city life would be
almost suicidal.

*Old age entails sacrifices of a kind that I would
not be brave enough to choose.*

March 15

I made my own some sentences of Canon Sheehan's
that I read years ago: "Now it seems to me a special
favor of Heaven that God should choose our sacrifices
for us. We have not the trouble of deliberating and
choosing, nor the fear that, after all, our sacrifices might
not prove acceptable. God has made the selection for us;

it only remains for us to accept His choice, and we are doing His will." Old age entails sacrifices of a kind that I would not be brave enough to choose. All that I can do is to pray to be sufficiently brave to accept what God has chosen, and trust Him to give me strength.

It is contact with real live persons
that the elderly crave.

March 16

Mrs. Donne asked Henry's advice, as she asks everybody's, apparently for the satisfaction of complaining about the amount of bad counsel she has had. He told her rather curtly to do something for others, and then came and told me of the incident. Now, it is easy enough to suggest to a recently widowed woman over seventy that she lose herself in serving others, but who wants her efforts? Her money, many could use gladly, of course, but I think it unlikely that many would brook her presence. And it is the loneliness, the sense of not being wanted or needed, of having no part in life, that are so hard to bear. There is, of course, a momentary pleasure in writing checks for charity, and there is a great comfort in the thought that one can do so rather than receive aid from others, but sitting at a desk writing checks is not the warm human occupation that the unimaginative may think. And it is contact with real live persons that the elderly crave. No matter how generously one gives or prays, to do so in solitude requires great faith. Had Mrs. Donne grandchildren, she could at least "baby-sit," for grandmothers have come into their own in servantless households, but she has nobody to serve, and, even if she had, her impaired hearing would handicap. The pity of her situation goes with me: there is so little left to attract: her charming appearance in middle-life somewhat compensated for her lack of personal magnetism. Her looks are gone, she is wraithe-like. Inclined to bitter speech, she repels acquaintances.

Discovering which acquaintances annoy me, I must endeavor to remember that these have a right to my instant prayer.

March 17

"By this shall all men know that you are My disciples, if you have love for one another." Loving everybody for God's sake, or at least trying to do so, I have a right to be articulate without shyness, for all forgive an older person for being ready to be kind and to say kind things; there is no danger of seeming forward or fulsome. I am free to love all as God's, and to pray Him to help them. Love through prayer, aid through prayer, no thought of any irksome person save coupled with prayer for that person. Discovering which acquaintances annoy me, I must endeavor to remember that these have a right to my instant prayer.

*[Trust] makes for a generous,
lighthearted gaiety.*

March 18

Trust does not preclude prudence, a thoughtful attitude to my problems, a strengthening of my reserves, but it does absolutely preclude solicitude in regard to my interior life. It makes for a generous, lighthearted gaiety, a Christian gaiety that is part of perfection because a manifestation of the happy relations between God and His creature.

[St. Joseph] had the virtues that the old need: faith, trust, an ability to remain in the background ready to serve.

March 19

I came across my Confirmation certificate that has lain for many years in the silver-chest. In a shaky foreign handwriting, it is inscribed, "Maria Joseph." Nobody would know it to be mine but St. Joseph and me. How little I dreamed as a child, when I insisted that I would have his name in Confirmation, that I, deemed so far from strong, would live to think him especially mine because a saint for the old! I believe it is said that he was not old, although artists usually portray him as grey-haired, but he had the virtues that the old need: faith, trust, an ability to remain in the background ready to serve. Small wonder that St. Teresa, who founded monasteries in poverty, looked to St. Joseph for sympathy and support. It is possible that much modern attachment to him is due to her writing. There was devotion before her day, but I like to think that he wanted very little expression in the early years of the Church lest some forget, in honoring the foster-father of Jesus, the divinity of One Who called Himself the Son of Man.

The clear-thinking Greeks knew what courage it took to face the vicissitudes of age.

March 20

I have just looked up A. E. Housman's translation[4] of a passage in Sophocles:

> For the years over-running the measure
>   Shall change thee in evil-wise:
> Grief draws nigh thee; and pleasure,
>   Behold, it is hid from thine eyes.

The clear-thinking Greeks knew what courage it took to face the vicissitudes of age. It is interesting to contrast their almost fatalistic attitude with the hope and faith of the Hebrew psalmist. There is a ruthlessness in Euripides' lines translated by C. M. Bowra:[5]

> Alas, how right the ancient saying is:
> We, who are old, are nothing else but noise
> And shape. Like mimicries of dreams we go,
> And have no wits, although we think us wise.

But David cried out energetically, "Cast me not off in the time of old age: when my strength shall fail, do not

---

[4] *Oxford Book of Greek Verse in Translation* (Oxford: Clarendon Press, 1938).
[5] *Ibid.*

thou forsake me." Again, "And unto old age and grey hairs: O God, forsake me not." And he declared of the just, "They shall still increase in a fruitful old age: and it shall be well with them. . . ." It is to Catholic Dante rather than to any ancient poet that we turn when seeking a phrase for our comfort: "In His will is our peace." The wearying years of probation. The will of God.

I think there are some people in the world who resent calm in others.

March 21

It is foolish to expect to be without the infirmity that comes with increasing age; having it, it is folly to deny it, to try to bluff about eyesight, or hearing or general strength. Honest acceptance is better.

Accepting human beings about us with clear knowledge of their limitations is indicated also. I remember Dick's saying lightheartedly that relatives furnished one's hair shirt. I think there are some people in the world who resent calm in others, and who have Puckish delight and ingenuity in surprising the would-be serene into sharp retort. No matter how determined I am, I am likely to be caught off-guard because I can not anticipate the angle of approach. Detachment, indifference, even Christian abandonment are what I need, of course, and knowing myself deficient in these, I must build up a little temporary defense.

I might fly to Rome.

March 22

The rock garden on the terrace close to the street gives me many occasions for pleasant chats, especially with passing children who pause to superintend my planting or to pick crocuses. But one of my most touching experiences of today was the comment of an old-rags-and-paper man, who was perched high on his dilapidated wagon. Checking his nag, he asked me, "Any junk?" I said that I had none, and then laughingly added, "Except me. I'm junk." His look of commiseration had a shade of heavenly pity, and just to show me that the whole world was kin, he assured me, "You're not half so much junk as me." The recollection of the kindly remark will be associated from now on, I suppose, with the tinkling bells of the collector and the call, "Any junk, today, any junk?"

I went there to dig because I wanted to think out my course in relation to Cecily. With life's experience to build on, it is not easy to forego advising the young, especially when their mistakes will cause them as well as me inconvenience. And the amount of self-control required to hold my tongue is equalled only by the generosity it takes to do so! Practically, I would not set so much store by silence did I not know that a question is posed by the needs of different generations. I may be wrong because behind the times. I was much struck when an elderly college trustee told me that whenever her judgment and that of younger members of the board differed, and the young carried the motion, she almost invariably decided later that they were right. The older member of a group is sometimes valuable as an anchor to youth's balloons, I suppose. But I think that the elderly are often too reluctant to trust, and so clutter endeavor. "If I can not help, I will not hinder" was a saying sweet to my ears when it suggested the withdrawal of my seniors. And when I voluntarily absent myself rather than be involved in discussion, I hope that my going gives pleasure and helps to clear the atmosphere.

My love can be without measure and my interest supreme, and yet it may be wise to express neither. To take the needs of others to the Holy Spirit by swift recourse to prayer is my office, and this in a quiet fashion, calling no attention to my exit. Perhaps my best solution would be to be off the scene. I might fly to Rome. Pneumonia used to be called the old people's friend before the miracle drugs were produced . . . but a modern invention, the aeroplane, undoubtedly is!

The punctual daffodils are pushing through the soil this morning.

March 23

The punctual daffodils are pushing through the soil this morning, and I have been thinking of my mother's delight in daffodils. All my life, I had heard her tell that when she was a child she would amuse herself in a corner of the garden where she was free to pick the flowers, and how the "butter-and-egg-flowers" were her favorites. One of the last years of her life, in the early spring, we drove to her childhood home, and straightway, when she got down from the car, she went to her play place. There, on the edge of a copse, in dazzling gold array, were the daffodils! For seventy years, at least, they had been multiplying themselves for a seventy-five-year-old lady's enchantment!

March 24

This is the anniversary of Cardinal Gibbons' death in 1921. He was eighty-seven years old, and I do not believe that he had ever been bored in his life. It was as a family friend that I knew him best and revered him, thinking little of his age or accomplishment. Now, of course, I know that he had a greater grasp of the potentialities existent in our Negro and immigrant populations than most reformers today dream; had he not been farsighted about their education, our problems would be even more serious than they are.

When I was at school, I used to look up and see him walking up the drive. And pretty soon we would be sent for. He always called to him all whose families had been known to him when he was Vicar Apostolic of North Carolina. The students broke into laughter when he described to me in their presence my grandfather's children: "Alice was beautiful. Lucy was brilliant. My child, you look like Lucy." He was seventy-six years old at that time, and, two years later, within a twelve-month period, confirmed seven thousand persons. I remember him sitting beside the altar rail in the Cathedral to hear confessions. And, always for me, "Lead, Kindly Light" is as much his hymn as Newman's, so frequently was it sung at his request. It is not strange that I should be thinking of him this evening, for I am considering a visit to Rome, and it is thanks to him that when I was first there as a child, garbed in white dress and veil, in the Sistine Chapel on Easter Sunday morning, I received our Lord from Pius X, the children's saint, the saint of the Holy Eucharist, and, by every right and title, one of God's blessed aged.

When I discover myself struggling against circumstances, I realize how much sheer bravery it takes to accept, to submit.

March 25

I have been sitting in the spring sunshine considering the joy that our Lord had in the sinlessness of our Lady. "Full of grace," she, His mother, was His fit companion. What must have been their conversations, His confidences, His assurances, her trust! I recall kneeling one Easter Sunday afternoon in the church of St. Severin in Paris (the white wings of the cornette of a Sister of Charity brushing me as I knelt). I was considering with delight the assertion just made in the *allocution* that the Resurrection news was no surprise to our Lady: her Son had greeted her first. The old abbé thought as I did. Learned though he was, his devotion was as simple as mine. When I reproach myself for lack of interest in popular modern novenas to our Lady, I comfort myself with the thought that my lifelong love of her as the sinless mother of Jesus, Mary "full of grace," is meaningful.

Our Lady's perfect humility sprang from her perfect faith: her *fiat* attested to her belief in the power of God. At the time of the Annunciation, she was not attempting great things. She was simply in God's presence when she consented to the overshadowing of the Holy Spirit. Her *fiat*, "Let it be done unto me according to Thy word," antedated her Son's prayer, "Thy will be done." And there is more fortitude than resignation evident in both utterances . . . fortitude and trust, faith, confidence, courage. When I discover myself struggling against circumstances, I realize how much sheer bravery it takes to accept, to submit. Glad, strong surrender I ask of myself these days: "Thy will be done."

I never know how to be honest and yet to seem to have an invariable Christian gaiety.

March 26

I am sorry to realize from Tom's reply that there was a note of depression in my recent letter. I never know how to be honest and yet to seem to have an invariable Christian gaiety. If I were perfect, I would be serene, even gay at all times. I face the fact that depression frequently results from physical weakness, and I am not surprised to be its victim on occasion, but, whenever I let it be seen that I am, I scandalize others. I ask help of the Holy Spirit, the Comforter, for I can understand that any melancholy shocks those who feel that they have the right to expect of every Christian, Christian gladness. Meanwhile, the letter-writing problem will be solved by means of postcards. There's not much room for low spirits on a postal!

Small as I am, I can in prayer lovingly embrace the universe.

March 27

Small as I am, I can in prayer lovingly embrace the universe. Jesus is not only my friend, I am also His. The obligation of friendship for His friends results. This means the prodigal giving of time and strength and thought for those known to me, and generous prayer for the entire world.

In a very minute fashion, my experience of Life enables me to succor others.

March 28

When we have lived long, we know so much of others' needs that we begin to appreciate the marvelous prevenience of Jesus. He was patient with the weak, mindful of the health of all. For instance, knowing Nicodemus' fear of the Sanhedrin, He received him after dark. He knew that Jairus' small daughter would be hungry, and bade her parents give her food; and that without the loaves and fishes, the fasting multitude would faint by the way. And mindful of the aching loneliness for His physical presence that would come to our Lady and St. John when He died, He gave them to each other as mother and son. In a very minute fashion, my experience of life enables me to succor others. I must live close enough to our Lord to note the opportunities.

A heart fused with our Lord's suffers as He did over the sins of mankind; . . . but, for the sinner, has mercy and compassion.

March 29

I want tolerance, mercy, unwillingness to condemn, to be evident in all my relations. "Neither do I condemn thee. . . ." And again, "Father, forgive them, for they know not what they do." Jesus knew that His persecutors could not comprehend what it was to crucify the Word. Sometimes I have been tempted to pray for those who made an old person's life more difficult: "Father, forgive them, for they know exactly what they do." Yet, in my heart I knew that the offenders forgot that their victim was God's child. When young persons pause to consider that, their patience with age is greater.

"The bruised reed he shall not break, and the smoking flax he shall not quench." A heart fused with our Lord's suffers as He did over the sins of mankind, suffers until it can barely endure its pain; but, for the sinner, has mercy and compassion. If my union with God were perfect, there would be no danger of the lapse from charity that is an outlet for human indignation. There would be no inner resentment. As it is, I judge too quickly and must be constantly on guard.

I have flown to Rome and back.

May 30

More than two months have passed since that last entry, for I have flown to Rome and back, seen some of the most beautiful countries of Europe from planes, and cruised through the Mediterranean and along the coast of Ireland. Such opportunities as I had seldom come the way of an individual, and I enjoyed the fine acting, rare music, and interesting personalities. I was conscious of a change in myself: my delight in everything lovely was intensified by the realization that it was passing. In other words, I am more than ever convinced that it is "towards evening" for me. Possibly that is why two moments stand out most clearly: that when I knelt for the blessing of His Holiness Pius XII, and thought how generously he gave of his strength. . . . "Unless the grain of wheat falling into the ground die, itself remaineth alone," and that immediately after, when I knelt in thanksgiving at the tomb of Pius X, the saint to whom I owe the privilege of daily Holy Communion.

There are seasons as we grow older characterized by a quiet silence. I look forward to one this summer.

May 31

I enjoy the tranquillity of our neighborhood after Easter: its calm is almost liturgical. A beautiful quiet marked the movements of our Lord after His Resurrection. On the Cross, He had cried out, "My God, my

God, why hast thou forsaken me?" And the earth had trembled with His agony. But, when He came to His disciples after the Resurrection, it was with such stillness that His very words had the quality of soothing silence. "Mary," He said to Mary Magdalen: and she needed no more. And, when the disciples were gathered together, He would be in their midst with no sound of arrival, "Peace be to you." There are seasons as we grow older characterized by a quiet silence. I look forward to one this summer.

It may not be as a soothing Comforter that the Holy Spirit comes.

June 1

Now there is a new poignancy in my relations with the Holy Spirit. The Third Person of the Blessed Trinity, Whose guidance I so sorely needed years ago, was too seldom invoked. In the hush of age, I shall beg Him to light the dimness.

I have been making the novena in preparation for Pentecost. Almost always, during a period of intensive prayer to the Holy Spirit, there has been light rather than sweetness, a terrible glare concentrated on my weaknesses, temptations, dangers; and any fault during those days has seemed to show up sin in its awfulness. Indeed, I do not remember a novena to the Holy Spirit not marked by such humiliation and suffering. But I can not let myself off because I am older, for now, more than ever, I need all those Sevenfold Gifts to make me ready for Heaven. It may not be as a soothing Comforter that the Holy Spirit comes, and, like other tired people, I want warmth and comfort. Nevertheless, I need light, and must dare pray with the Church:

> *Veni, Sancte Spiritus*
> *Et emitte cœlitus*
> *Lucis tuæ radium.*

And then:

> Heal our wounds, our strength renew
> On our dryness pour Thy dew
> Wash the stains of guilt away.
> Bend the stubborn heart and will:
> Melt the frozen, warm the chill:
> Guide the steps that go astray.

New beginnings are necessary now. I must arrange a new schedule as calmly as I would have worked out a more ambitious one in my youth. Prayer must have more place in it. Listening is now more important than teaching or other active employment, for, if I listen, I become a sort of clearing house for young ambitions, ventures, dreams. Years ago, one June evening, I was watching the pigeons swirl over the city roofs, and hearing the bells of a neighboring church. I was unwillingly giving my attention to another's talk, when it came over me that, whereas I could not answer the summons to Benediction, I could listen to the narrator in union with the Sacred Heart. And there was borne in on me a new estimate of the value of kindly listening, a thought that has stood me in good stead throughout my life. We can listen to others gladly as God does to us.

Christ was invariably specially kind to individuals whom He was called on to judge.

June 2

From day to day and year to year, I set higher value on the virtue of kindness . . . plain, ordinary everyday kindness in any dealing with any human being of any race or creed. Kindness is so essential to true justice that I feel it to be part of it. When I approach a situation gently, my mind remains clear. It seems to me that Christ was invariably specially kind to individuals whom He was called on to judge. The classic example, of course, was His quietly writing in the dust while the woman and her accusers awaited His word: giving all time to think, to examine their consciences. But there were many other occasions in the Gospels when He showed Himself kind first, then acted as was best. A person who reaches my age has to face a record of many shortcomings, to be sorry for many faults: but any act of unkindness in my past life certainly calls for particular contrition now. The most harm that most of us have done is due, I think, to deficiency in a virtue that is not necessarily even Christian, a natural virtue.

June 3

I have been rejoicing in union with the Heart of Jesus, thinking of our Lord's delight in the goodness of those at Mass this morning, the First Friday in June.

*Acceptance [is] a more attractive virtue
than resignation.*

June 4

Sometimes, in God's Providence, a joyous peace comes to us when we feel lonely and abandoned. Merely the peace that follows defeat, perhaps; it is not built entirely on weak surrender, however, but on crushed pride and ambition, conquered restlessness. It belongs to acceptance, a more attractive virtue than resignation. Enjoying such moments, the aged are like the psalmist who, not forgetting to bewail past sins, nor unmindful of the potentiality to sin again, gloried in God's mercy of the moment.

*The teaching of the Church on the Holy Spirit's
indwelling heartens the lonely.*

June 5

Pentecost Sunday. I am thankful to have made the novena to the Holy Spirit. I doubt if any young person knows how, having passed middle-age convinced of one's ignorance as to one's course, it becomes second nature to implore His guidance. He is the Comforter, especially in age, when one needs light and warmth and love, His attributes. And the teaching of the Church on His indwelling heartens the lonely. To be in a state of grace is to have His companionship.

Always there lingers the ambition to serve others.

June 7

Alone before the Blessed Sacrament yesterday, I made an act of acceptance of my curiously lonely and unexpected manner of living. Always there lingers the ambition to serve others. Surely, if ever anyone was a Mary because our Lord would have it so, I am. He chose the best part for me: it would not have occurred to me to do so. To correspond with His grace by spending my time in prayer rather than in the corporal works of mercy is to be well-balanced rather than eccentric. I think of Blessed Robert Southwell's writing, when he was a mere lad, that he must remember when he was at prayer that nothing else that he could be doing would be what he was fit to do at that moment.

The destitute have a good chance to arrive in Heaven before they are admitted to a Home on Earth.

June 9

One day, when I was young and persuasive, the secretary of an organized charity asked me to call on an old woman who lived alone in rooms in a tenement, and explain to her that the society would no longer countenance paying her rent, it being deemed unwise for her to be solitary. I was to convince her that an old people's home was the best solution.

She considered the matter politely, and firmly refused. Casting about for some expedient, I asked, "Wouldn't

Father Giles at St. Clare's pay your rent?"

"Him?" she retorted, "Him? He's all for the children! Oh well, put my name on the Little Sisters' list, if you want to. It's long. I may die before I get there."

I could well understand Father Giles' being all for the children. And I thoroughly sympathized with the old woman's method of ridding herself of me. And, unfortunately, she was stating the truth when she mentioned the length of waiting lists for institutions for the aged. Places are scarce even for those who can afford to pay, and the destitute have a good chance to arrive in Heaven before they are admitted to a Home on Earth.

Hope, natural in youth, is essential in age.

June 10

Hope, natural in youth, is essential in age. While I await the time of God's good pleasure, I trust Him. Now I must have that meekness with myself that St. Francis de Sales urged on his penitents, not brooding on the mistakes of my life, but making allowances for the impetuousness of youth as God did.

June 11

If I could choose but two of the longer ejaculations that the Church offers us for use, my selection would be, "Holy, holy, holy Lord God of Hosts, all the earth is full of Thy glory. Glory be to the Father and to the Son and to the Holy Ghost," and, "Jesus meek and humble of

Heart, make our hearts like unto Thine." Praise of the Trinity. Appeal to the Heart of Christ.

I like to think of the perfection of the idea of God as a Trinity.

June 12

This is Trinity Sunday. For years and years I have known its Mass almost by heart. I, who can understand so little of the mystery celebrated today, love it nevertheless. I like to think of the perfection of the idea of God as a Trinity. I cannot state my thought exactly, but there is a generosity in make-up, so to speak, in the reciprocal love of Three Persons, that one can not imagine love as having without this triune feature. The Father, Son, and Holy Ghost loving Each Other.

Forever, I associate the Athanasian Creed, recited at Prime today, with little Aunt Lucy's last illness. She was eighty-eight, and had cancer. We were beside her bed. She began to ask different members of the household, "Do you believe?" somewhat as the question had been asked by the Evangelicals who surrounded her in a plantation childhood. Then her blue eyes blazing, her voice strong, she recited the Creed of St. Athanasius. I could scarcely credit my ears when the verses followed on one another: "But the Godhead of the Father, and of the Son, and of the Holy Ghost is but one, the glory equal, and the majesty coeternal." Faith had come to her, through God's grace, by conquest. Somehow, it seemed a testimony to her battle for it that she, at her advanced age, remembered this Creed word for word.

*With my temperament, 'busy work' serves
no purpose.*

June 13

I have been sitting with Mrs. Carew on her verandah.
I like to see an elderly person placidly knitting, as she
was, even if the garment produced seems to me hideous
and of no value. With my temperament, "busy work" of
that kind serves no purpose. But the employment that
old people find for themselves soothes them, and keeps
them out of the way, just as making scrapbooks does
children.

I have decided that the best attitude to "busy work"
for the aged is one of *laisser faire*. I would be irritated by
being expected to knit for the therapeutic value of the
occupation. I prefer the Biblical right of the old, to
"dream dreams" with my hands idle.

*At last, too old for his active apostolate in
the streets, he had leisure for uninterrupted
contemplation.*

June 14

On other visits to Rome, I have failed, for one reason
or another, to reach St. Philip Neri's tiny chapel, close to
the roof-tops of the Chiesa Nuova. But this year, the sacristan took me there alone. I have been thinking of the
holy old saint celebrating Mass. From his altar, he could
see the Janiculum Hill on which he had "made himself a
child with the children"; and stretching out below was
the Rome that he loved. But now that he could linger as

long as he liked at Mass, I doubt if he thought of his lads
of the Oratory or even his beloved city, for the Host held
in his fragile old hands was God, Whom he would soon
see face to face. At last, too old for his active apostolate
in the streets, he had leisure for uninterrupted contemplation. Truly such leisure is one of the delights of being
old.

June 15

I have been trying to pray for Charles. Almost my only
means of help is generous prayer. I know the uselessness
of interposing, and believe the worth of absolute silence
to be greater than expressions of opinions that the young
will revel in disregarding as old-fashioned. If we consider
our Lord's methods, we note that He did not coerce.
Tact, sympathy, charitable reticence marked His dealings. He gave all the privilege of free will.

*The Holy Eucharist is the great bond
of union for Catholics.*

June 16

Corpus Christi. I knelt last at the altar rail, which was
so angled that I saw other communicants as the priest
advanced with the ciborium. Each, waiting with folded
hands, was known to the Lord and knew Him. Again I
thought of how the Holy Eucharist is the great bond of
union for Catholics. No matter how we differ in worldly
position or intellectual attainments, we find ourselves

caught up in this great mystery of faith together. And we remember that our being together at the altar rail gives joy to Jesus, Whose delight is to be with the children of men.

The literary life can be holy.

June 17

So many young people are eager to write. The literary life can be holy. To begin with, the long hard pull, and the willingness to test accomplishment by the criticism of others and yet retain faith in one's individual talent, beget humility. It takes more courage to throw the results of agonizing effort on the mercy of a literate but half-educated public than was required of the ancients, whose works could be circulated in manuscript in a chosen group. Whereas writing for oneself may cater to one's feeling of self-importance with none of the soul-forming discipline that comes to the published writer willy-nilly, writing to be read, with a given audience to inform, is an unselfish vocation. So often when I look at a book, I think of the hours and hours of hard labor that went to the making of it.

For a person whose death can not be far off, this glad account of making ready for Heaven is excellent reading.

June 18

It is very hot, and I have done little but read. I have spent many hours on the martyrs' letters published by the Catholic Record Society of London. I hope that the day will come when the English-speaking world will know more about the young English Martyrs. Our reluctance to consider the religious persecutions of the Tudor reigns is natural, but the joyful heroism of the youths trained on the Continent for the English mission was such that their fate scarcely saddens. The students at the English College at Rome knew that when they returned to England, they would in all likelihood be captured, imprisoned, and hanged, for, under the Act of 1585, any native-born subject of the Queen who had been ordained a Roman Catholic priest since the first year of her accession, and resided in England more than forty days, was guilty of treason and incurred the penalty of death. My mind reverts again and again to my stay in Rome in the spring, and to my search for places associated with the martyrs there and in London. The holiness of Robert Southwell is evident in all that he wrote and did. The editor of the diary that he kept when a student in Rome has written that it is one of the most remarkable records of the formation of a martyr's soul. Certainly, for a person whose death can not be far off, this glad account of making ready for Heaven is excellent reading. I was struck by lines in Blessed Ralph Sherwin's letter, written after his indictment and shortly before his martyrdom. He was in chains in his London prison. "I wear now on my feet and hands some little bells to keep me in mind who I am. Pray for me that I may finish my course with courage and fidelity." And later, "Delay of our death doth somewhat dull me. It was not without cause that our Master said, '*Quod facis, fac cito.*'"

God knows what my limitations were.

June 19

God sees the old not as childish, but as what they have been, are, and will be, His children. He makes allowances for the past and does not forget what the elderly sinner is too apt to forget, the circumstances of temptation, the pitfalls on the way to spiritual triumph. Looking back regretfully, I wonder why such a mistaken course, but God knows what my limitations were. On the other hand, it seems to me that He expects me to demand of myself the ultimate of which He and I know me to be capable. Some of my associates might excuse me from effort because of my years, and it is a temptation to avail myself of their leniency, but if I am gentle and firm with myself, I can continue the struggle for perfection. "Continue" seems hardly the word for something forever beginning!

June 20

I spent last evening reading *King Lear.* Even when I was young, it seemed to me the greatest of the tragedies. Now I am amused to note that my sympathy, once almost entirely with Cordelia, has shifted somewhat to the unworldly old king. Not enough, however, to cause me to doubt that, in Cordelia's place, I would have behaved exactly as she did!

June 21

A letter from Margaret informs me that she plans to bring her grandchildren, aged seven and eight, for a visit.

I know my inability and this should prevent my being stupid enough to be proud.

June 22

I have wondered that I did not accuse myself of pride as often as formerly, and I realize that age in itself furnishes some correctives. I know my inability and this should prevent my being stupid enough to be proud. But I must cultivate humility and lowliness: I must learn to love my weakness because it teaches me to consider my littleness, my utter dependence on God, my place among His creatures. Contemplating Jesus as He tells us to do, we learn His meekness and humility. The strength of Jesus is at our disposal: He gives it to us to fortify our frailty.

Often, these days, I make a conscious act of humility when speaking or writing. I know that my expression may provoke condemnation of me, perhaps as a meddlesome woman, overzealous, nonconformist, no matter what; but if there is something worthwhile at stake, the little sacrifice of my vanity is nothing to grudge.

As I get older, I consider very often [St. John the Baptist's] saying, when referring to Jesus: 'He must increase, and I decrease.'

June 24

I do not think that most moderns have an intelligent love of St. John the Baptist—partly, no doubt, because we, who have lived through two world wars, have found our penance ready-made, and subconsciously have been repelled by the idea of voluntary penance that John the Baptist urged. But our Lord said that there was not born a greater than John. Certainly, as I get older, I consider very often his saying, when referring to Jesus, "He must increase, and I decrease," or, as Monsignor Knox rendered it, "He must grow more and more, and I less and less." When I try to be more mindful of God than of me, when I commit an undertaking to the Holy Spirit as self forgetfully as possible, myself but an awkward instrument, I ask St. John's aid. I have often thought of the wonderful aptness with which the Church applies to him the words of Isaias, "a chosen arrow." Had that rendering been in the King James Version rather than in the Douay, it would have been snatched up as a title by one of the playwrights forever tempted by the story of the Precursor. What an excellent title "A Chosen Arrow" would be!

*God has not let me experience the sense of
desolation that He permits the strong.*

June 26

My birthday. I read the Book of Job as usual. Surely, for
one who has suffered, forever upheld by God, never
tempted to doubt His mercy and His wisdom, this is perfect birthday reading. God has not let me experience the
sense of desolation that He permits the strong. When I
knew myself the weakest, His power was my refuge. I
trust that, if He wills to withdraw the light and leave me
in seeming darkness, He will give grace for the trial.

*Catherine of Siena had first-hand knowledge of the
trial that an old parent can be.*

June 27

Today, reading Terce and Sext for Monday, I chided
myself with David's words, "Wait on the Lord, do manfully, and let thy heart take courage; and wait thou on
the Lord." "Do ye manfully and let your heart be
strengthened: all ye that hope in the Lord." How often
my little Catherine of Siena quoted those lines! I can
almost see her dictating them in a letter to Pope Gregory
XI. Catherine, by the way, had first-hand knowledge of
the trial that an old parent can be, for Monna Lapa, her
crotchety old mother, was not willing for her to be out
of her sight. Monna Lapa must have been somewhat of
an incubus for Catherine's secretaries; they have not
given her a reputation for sanctity. It is said that Lapa
had had twenty-five children, but Catherine, whose

mission it was to bring peace to the Church, was the one whom she elected to follow even to Rome. Naturally enough, of course, for Catherine was the only saint in the lot.

June 28

A modern scientist has explained why time seems to pass more quickly as we age. I do not understand the relation of this appearance to the physiological processes, but I do know that the rushing days, really given us to make ready for Heaven, seem so short that they tempt us to procrastinate.

So often, I feel that I have labored and taken nothing, that I am weary and defeated.

June 29

I have always loved St. Peter because our Lord did, and because He chose him, in all his apparent weakness, to be the rock on which His Church was founded. But, of late years, I have come to love him for his saintly qualities: his literalness, simplicity, fervor. Our Lord made use of his literalness, as He did of the same quality in Martha, to teach some of the most sublime truths of the Faith. "Thou art the Christ," St. Peter affirmed. And when Jesus asked if they would desert, he answered, "Lord, to whom shall we go? Thou hast the words of eternal life." But perhaps it is in all that he has to teach the old that I have come to understand him best. When he had labored all night long and taken nothing, he was still willing to let down his net at the command of Jesus. So often, I feel that I have labored and taken nothing, that I am weary and defeated; it has not seemed God's design to answer my prayer in my way, even when that prayer was for the conversion of those who were, by every right, His. Then, in obedience, faith, trust, I try to launch out into the deep again and make a new beginning. There were times when Peter failed signally, too, but never a time when he did not love and repent. He and St. Thomas had, it seems to me, a greater struggle for faith than any of the apostles, but they were so generous in their effort, so quick to try to follow in spite of their lack of ability to do so, that our Lord employed their very failures for His ends. Peter must have been young when fishing on Genesareth; he was old when martyred at Rome. I was thinking just then, of the curious *Quo Vadis* legend, and of how it points up, as the Gospels do, Peter's dependence on Christ.

June 30

So frequent was the quoting of St. Paul in our household that some passages come to memory in the very intonations of different members of the family. (If in the King James Version rather than in the Douay, the sense of the sayings was usually the same.) One that means the most for me, who find meditation time a period of wrestling with the desire not to meditate, a fight against ennui, distractions, everything . . . is his prayer that his disciples "be strengthened by His Spirit with might unto the inward man." Most human wills are very strong, mine included, and, with God's strength added, there is hope for victory.

I am dry, distracted, and humanly lonely.

July 1

Not only do I usually feel stronger in summer than during other seasons, but I have more time for prayer. I was impressed once by hearing in a sermon in a vacation resort chapel, "Summer time is sin time." It must have been then that, understanding the temptations to laxity that prevail during days of idleness, I realized that summer must be my season for reparation. In winter, I can do little but bear with the cold and the inconveniences incident to it, but in summer, it is easy enough to make an extra visit to the Blessed Sacrament, or to sit quietly on the porch in the twilight with my rosary in my hand. When I wonder if I am overbold to think of any prayer of mine as prayer of reparation, I remember that it is my only service these days and that our Lord let repentant sinners serve: Magdalen, by using her as an example of love's power: poor, denying Peter: doubting Thomas. Weak as I am, I love Him, and so, in loving all the world with Him, uniting my love to that of others that may not be expressed in formal prayer, my prayer may partake, in a manner, of reparation. I do not know. But, through July, when many are not so mindful of prayer or the sacraments as they might be, I shall offer my acts of love as part of all beings' adoration: complementing, perhaps, rather than supplementing. I am dry, distracted,

and humanly lonely. But if I make use of the means at
hand, the oblivion, the quiet, the opportunities for recollection, this summer will be a period of retreat and calm
happiness.

*It has always seemed to me that those not attracted
to the cloister have, as their first duty, kindness to
their God-given kin.*

July 2

The Visitation, the first recorded work of charity of
our Blessed Mother, was a kindness to one of her own
kindred, St. Elizabeth. It was our Lord's own cousin,
John the Baptist, whom He sanctified before his birth. It
was the privilege of Elizabeth to testify to the presence of
Jesus and to call forth from Mary the *Magnificat*.

It has always seemed to me that those not attracted to
the cloister have, as their first duty, kindness to their
God-given kin. Their relationship does not change as they
grow older, for, as the family group shrinks, the need for
the individuals' help is intensified: the kind of service is
different, but the duty remains. When I see good people
busy about works for organized charity, I often think of
members of their immediate families tucked away in run-
down boarding houses and nursing homes. Had those,
who are now occupied with elaborate efforts for the wel-
fare of the aged indigent, been trained to see their own
connections as their first and holiest duty, public institutions would be less crowded. I grant that there would be
more saints, for nobody is as exacting as one's kin, and in
no circumstances do greater difficulties present themselves

than in nursing one's own family. But in this country, many shift onto the shoulders of the public problems that might be handled at home. From the spiritual angle, members of one's family are truly God's, and He is served in giving them the cup of water in His name.

Our thrush's song is, I think, as beautiful as the nightingale's.

July 3

Deliberately, I have sought no companionship over the weekend, spoken agreeably when addressed, let little Jane sit here and cut paper-dolls, but avoided conversation with anyone. This is the nearest to retreat that my life affords, and is seldom possible save in hot summer weather such as we have been having. I was awake at dawn. The birds were singing, and I lay listening to their chorus. The clear note of the thrush was loveliest, as always. Our thrush's song is, I think, as beautiful as the nightingale's. This morning, recalling St. Francis de Sales' illustration in *The Treatise on the Love of God,* I substituted my thrush for his *maître rossignol,* and delighted all the more in the melody. That passage is one of the most charming in St. Francis' writings.

When I hear the thrushes, I think of my mother. She loved the sound of running water, children's voices, and the song of the thrush. Even before she was old, she was denied them by the loss of her hearing, and when she would note my attention to the little boys' prattle, or my pause to listen to a singing thrush, a sweet smile of recognition would come.

*I delight in the thought that our Lord spent His
life in a lovely land.*

July 5

I have been recalling the natural beauty of many
places associated with the saints: Rome, Assisi, Siena,
Paris, Rouen, Lisieux, St. Paul's Athens, the English
Martyrs' Surrey, and Lake George, the Lake of the
Blessed Sacrament, so dear to St. Isaac Jogues. I delight
in the thought that our Lord spent His life in a lovely
land, that He could watch the purple shadows on the
Plain of Esdraelon, and gaze on the mountains that rise
from it. Doubtless, when on the Sea of Galilee with His
apostles, He sometimes raised His eyes from their
brown, weather-beaten faces to observe the light play on
the brilliant snows of Hermon. The *Benedicite* was His
before it was ours.

*Everything is simplified when laid before Jesus
with the assurance that He has the answer.*

July 6

"Lord, to Whom shall we go? Thou hast the words of
eternal life." St. Peter's reply to our Lord is forever in my
thoughts these days. Truly, to whom shall we go save
Christ as we age? Even if not neglected or repudiated by
others, we are ourselves convinced that others have not
leisure for us. Any problem that besets us is our own: its
solution matters not a whit to an outsider. Whenever I
consider consulting this person or that, I come to St.
Peter's conclusion. Everything is simplified when laid

before Jesus with the assurance that He has the answer.

I can understand that I might seem morbid did I state that I had no expectation of help in ordinary matters, for I know that, in acute distress, I would be relieved. But it is the small daily puzzles that I turn over to our Lord.

It was wise not to send more than a brief note in reply to Charles' letter. In this instance, aloofness as an expression of human dignity will effect more than words. I acknowledge my helplessness before God, and ask Him to supply for me any conciliatory gesture that I might make. It seems to me best to accept the fact that anything that I say might make matters worse. It is hard to admit defeat, but the defeat is mine, not God's. The privilege of expressing my loving interest has been denied me; but I can still love and be interested, leaving all initiative to the Holy Spirit. In the end, the decades of effort will not have been wasted.

July 14

I have not opened this book for a week. My seven- and eight-year-old visitors and their grandmother left on the noon train. It took an extra piece of luggage for the booty, which included a small baseball bat. Having been schooled to pitch that a catcher might practice, I picked up where I left off about four decades ago. We fed swan and deer, and tried all the swings and see-saws within reach. When it rained, and they were tired of coloring pictures, I read aloud. The few children's books that remain on the shelves were a treasure-trove. Curiously enough, for they are thorough moderns, they enjoyed best "A Midsummer Night's Dream" and "King Lear" in Lamb's *Tales from Shakespeare*. To them, the ass's head was high comedy, and the kindness of Kent nearly brought tears. Their grandmother asked me to take them to church with me. Unfortunately, the Catholic practice that appealed to them was lighting candles. They did so at such a rate that a conflagration seemed imminent, and I lost track of the number of intentions. I put money in the box, but I had not enough to pay for their inroads on the supply.

That I am weary, goes without saying. But I am glad that they came.

I had not Teresa's understanding of the awfulness of sin, but sufficient intelligence to avoid some of my shortcomings.

July 17

Yesterday I was reading St. Teresa's *Autobiography,* and it occurred to me that God gives me the saints' writings as mirrors in which I see my ugly self. Teresa was analytical, slow in reaching perfection, entirely aware of her faults yet weak in the struggle against them, so conscious of God's glorious beauty that her own venial sins stood out like dark splotches against a background of light. She, perhaps more than any woman writer, draws me to look at my own soul objectively. Yesterday, as I read, a new horror of my tarnishing faults came to me, especially of the imperfections to which I have yielded because I relished them, words of criticism uttered not spontaneously but after consideration, words that I might have checked. The wilfulness that went into my wrongdoing I knew all the while: I had not Teresa's understanding of the awfulness of sin, but sufficient intelligence to avoid some of my shortcomings.

I am thankful that I have had the saints' own writings to read rather than writings about them. I had read St. Teresa's *Autobiography* because it was at hand long before I ever read a biography of her. It seems to me that, as a rule, it is best to let the saints, and especially the mystics, speak for themselves. For one thing, so few hagiographers are holy enough to understand a saint's mind, and very few sufficiently gifted to describe what they do understand. There are exceptions, of course: books such as Edmund Gardner's *Life of St. Catherine of Siena*, that are masterpieces; but, on the whole, letters and notes, prefaced by an account of the circumstances of their composition, make better reading.

I believe that in my relations with my family, it is well to bear in mind God's manner of dealing with me.

July 18

I believe that in my relations with my family, it is well to bear in mind God's manner of dealing with me. He bestows on me free will. If I misuse this, He stands ready to succor and forgive. I must, as a rule, allow others freedom in their decisions, trusting God to give me strength to help them if they make mistakes. I, too, might err in a course that I would choose for them, and my prevenient attitude might be the wrong one. I must have the courage to sacrifice my judgment, even if I feel reasonably certain that their unwise choice will entail difficulty for me. This calls for unselfishness and confidence that only those who have paid the price often can estimate.

I am especially attracted by the saints remarkable for their common sense.

July 19

Perhaps it is because it has been necessary for me to be practical that I am especially attracted by the saints remarkable for their common sense. My original interest in St. Vincent de Paul, whose feast this is, began with the reading of a sociologist's dissertation on his charities. I was particularly struck by the arrangements that he made for impoverished elderly couples to continue their life together. For the war-stricken, he provided food first, then seed that they might raise their own grain and bring plenty back to their devastated fields. That he was holy as well as practical, I could not doubt, for, had he not been, St. Francis de Sales, who knew souls so well, would not have entrusted to him the spiritual direction of his Paris convent of the Visitation. All of this, I have pondered for years, but this hot evening sitting on the porch in the dark, I have been recalling St. Vincent's last days at Saint-Lazare. He, who had ridden horseback far and wide to visit his country missions, was constrained to make use of a little carriage; then, finally, he was confined to an armchair and nursed as an invalid. Having done so much for the old, he suffered old age himself, and lived to be almost eighty. Formerly, there was some doubt about the date of his birth, but, with this now established as about 1581, his death in 1660 entitles him to a high place among my old saints.

July 20

Now Thabor, now Gethsemane. How many times during our lives we have gone from one to the other. On Thabor, we have glimpsed the beauty of Heaven: encouraged, elated, we have thought, "It is good for us to be here." Then, we have been plunged in the sorrow of Gethsemane. As we grow old, we are at home in either place. In Gethsemane, too, we can say, "It is good for us to be here," for we have learned to say, "Thy will be done."

July 21

For years, I have meditated on our Lord's warnings against solicitude. Recently I have become aware that there can be a solicitude that is not concerned with material or intellectual endeavor, a sort of spiritual fussiness . . . a worry about perfection that is incompatible with confidence.

*Just as Your Lord chose weak Peter for his faith,
so He chose erring Magdalen for her love.*

July 22

Our Lord's treatment of Mary Magdalen can not be truly understood by a young person, I imagine. More and more, I see that His dealing with her was for our therapy as well as hers. Through His forgiveness, His gentleness, His permitting her to lavish love that to others seemed too human, He showed the great mercy of His heart. It was her brother Lazarus whom He raised from the dead. It was to her that He appeared at the tomb. Just as He chose weak Peter for his faith, so He chose erring Magdalen for her love, once that love was directed towards Himself.

I used to watch young men, all men, indeed, shy off from an aging woman. Now, I shy first!

July 23

I am amused by the comfort that I take in remembering how my companions and I regarded older people. I note now that others, especially men, appraise my years, and are tolerant even as we were. Polite, if the society of our elders was unavoidable, we evaded it whenever possible. I used to watch young men, all men, indeed, shy off from an aging woman. Now, I shy first! If sought for any reason, I try to be serenely nonassertive. The repetitions of the ancients were anathema to me once and. . . . Well, why pursue the subject? Suffice it to say that not the least important of my resolutions for my last years is to be little in evidence.

July 24

Cousin Jessie has been here for a visit. At seventy-nine, she is wonderful. Interested in people and clothes, especially her own clothes and the care of her appearance, she is a delightful person to have in the house. She has lived in the country and has always been poor, and this was her first visit. It seemed wise to sense what she really wanted to see in the city and to limit our expeditions. We made the rounds of the shops with the old names, those from which purchases were made by mail when she was a girl in the South. "Mama always trusted this shop," she would say as we roamed the aisles of one of the oldest department stores. She insisted on visiting the Cathedral, partly as a tribute to my faith, no doubt. I did not mention the Art Museum. Nor dared I say "Zoo," lest she should want to visit it in order to describe the animals to her small grandson.

Homes for the aged are full of old people who have been urged to go in peace when they knew not where to go.

July 25

Fidelity in an extraordinary degree marks the saints, I suppose, and a lack of it, whether in great matters or small, marks the rest of us. The saints are in Heaven because they have been faithful to God: the souls banished to Purgatory are there purely and simply because they have not corresponded with the grace given them: because, wilfully or carelessly, they have been unfaithful.

Sometimes it seems to me that the commonsense road

to sanctity is nowhere better pointed out than in St. James' Epistle. Meditated and lived, it would make saints of us. Those of us who have wrestled with human nature, its foibles and self-deceptions, find many a temptation incident to ordinary life in the world dealt with by St. James. "But if any man think himself religious, not bridling his tongue but deceiving his own heart, this man's religion is vain. Religion clean and undefiled before God and the Father is this: to visit the fatherless and widows in their tribulation and keep one's self unspotted from the world." Nothing could be more practical than that. And, which of us having received advice and no help, can refrain from quoting to ourselves the verses: "And if a brother or sister be naked and want daily food: And one of you say to them: Go in peace, be ye warmed and filled; yet give them not those things that are necessary for the body, what shall it profit?" Monsignor Knox's version is as stark as the Douay: "Here is a brother, here is a sister, going naked, left without means to secure daily food; if one of you says to them, Go in peace, warm yourselves and take your fill, without providing for their bodily needs, of what use is it?"

Homes for the aged are full of old people who have been urged to go in peace when they knew not where to go.

*There is great rest in recognizing that I need
express no opinion as a rule, and am free to keep
my counsel, protecting myself thus from wearying
friction and not adding to general turmoil.*

July 26

This is Saint Anne's feast. Our old Italian pastor used
to refer to her as "Our Lord's Grandmother." I took my
neighbors' grandmother to Mass, they being on vacation. I remarked her self-control, for, for the first time, I
talked with her enough to note that she is not blind to
things as they are. She is far on in her seventies, and,
although not necessarily uncritical, she is reticent for the
sake of peace. "Peace, peace, peace," we may all say
these days as Catherine of Siena repeated her "*Pace,
pace, pace.*" The part that we older people have in the
world's peace is perhaps a passive one, but an addition
to the modicum existent. For myself, there is great rest in
recognizing that I need express no opinion as a rule, and
am free to keep my counsel, protecting myself thus from
wearying friction and not adding to general turmoil.

July 31

I wish I might find a biography of St. Ignatius Loyola
that roused me to a love of him. He was a friend of my
St. Philip Neri, so I ought to love him for that alone. And
to the French Jesuits, his followers, I am forever indebt-
ed. I have always doubted his being a particularly mag-
netic saint; but perhaps he deliberately hid that quality.
He recognized it in another, evidently. It is said that he
was so attracted to St. Philip Neri that he held him by a

button of his cassock on a Roman street corner, lest he slip away. Characteristically, St. Philip solved the problem by leaving the button with St. Ignatius, and going off to his boys of the Oratory.

The young and strong can nurse the sick; but we, feeble and weary, can comfort the sorrowful, for we, knowing sorrow, know sympathy.

August 1

Occasionally, we have the privilege of letting another ease a troubled mind by talking to us. To listen quietly in union with our Lord is to share the habitual charity of God, Who forever listens to us all. Listening is, in a way, an adjunct to counselling the doubtful, one of the Spiritual Works of Mercy. It is the Spiritual rather than the Corporal Works that remain for us. The young and strong can nurse the sick; but we, feeble and weary, can comfort the sorrowful, for we, knowing sorrow, know sympathy.

Shared pain is somehow like shared bread, it brings its participants closer to each other.

August 2

I have been reading about St. Alphonsus Liguori. He has never attracted me as some saints have, but Newman's references to him, his admiration for him, and his doubt that he thoroughly understood the saint's Latin temperament, awakened my interest. Surely nobody could fail to be touched by the sufferings of this holy man who lived to be ninety-one. A severe attack of illness in middle life had left his head bent, his chin pressed against his chest. He could drink from the chalice at Mass only when aided by an acolyte, and at meals, employed a drinking tube. He was under the Pope's disapproval because, unwittingly, he had signed a revised rule not sanctioned by the authorities. Moreover, for several years, he was tormented by religious doubt. Two kinds of hardship that would test a vigorous man. Yet, he persevered. Occasionally there comes to me the thought that God trusts the holy old enough to give them a particular passion: He knows what they can endure for Him. Shared pain is somehow like shared bread, it brings its participants closer to each other, and the saints who have had a special agony in their last years are dear to me whether they were old or young. Doubtless Newman's extreme sensitiveness to the distrust of his critics, Catholic and Protestant alike, begot his sympathy for St. Alphonsus.

Beset by temptations to pride, bitterness, and other sins to which the lonely are liable, I am thankful that, having no audience, I am not giving scandal by expressing my feelings.

August 3
Solitude is sometimes a spiritual asset for a noncontemplative. Too quick to speak, my tongue has been the instrument of sin, uncharitable speech, complaints. When I am alone, I have no need to use it for good or

evil, and, in silent thought, I consider how I am being spared an opportunity to sin. Beset by temptations to pride, bitterness, and other sins to which the lonely are liable, I am thankful that, having no audience, I am not giving scandal by expressing my feelings. It is, I admit, a negative sort of comfort in desolation, but, for one who loves God, it works for good. And there is a positive side to it—leisure for acts of contrition and repentance for sins of the tongue, a prelude to Extreme Unction.

My being on earth, useless and perhaps burdensome to others, is not my fault.

August 4
    In the loneliness of today, I must try to think of myself not at all save as God's. I need not be discouraged by failures past or present, or wearied by ambition to help except through prayer. I exist because it is God's will that I exist. My being on earth, useless and perhaps burdensome to others, is not my fault. I do not understand, but perhaps my soul will be brightened by this tarrying in earthly trial. Somehow, rightly used, this time will serve to chasten me and make me more pleasing to God. The habit of trust is not entirely mine yet, but I know that even in a worldly way everything that is not preparation for Heaven is useless to me, there being no worldly success possible.

August 5

I have thought so much this week of the quiet of our Lord, of His gentleness and tranquillity, of His waiting so many years to begin His Public Life and then working serenely, unhurriedly.

August 6

When our Lord took Peter and James and John to Mount Thabor and was transfigured before them, He was Himself no different from usual. What He did was to permit His apostles to see Him as He was.

I try . . . to leave all to God, to have no fretful worry, no anxiety, no solicitude.

August 7

I have found great comfort in the habit of daily offering chaplets of the Rosary for persons and causes dear to my heart. The Joyful Mysteries every day for Mollie, the Sorrowful for Cecily, and the Glorious for Charles, whose primary need is faith, and who so loves beauty as to be attracted by the beauty attached to our Faith. I try, in praying these chaplets, to leave all to God, to have no fretful worry, no anxiety, no solicitude. Had I not suffered so long and so fruitlessly for each, I would not have found this definite prayer for each such a solace. As it is, I endeavor to forget the need in praying the Mystery, and the prayer thus becomes a restful act of charity.

Hundreds of others are serving God,
having offered their good works for His glory,
but I have leisure for the quiet prayer of praise
and thanksgiving.

August 8

Now and then sitting alone, I remember that I am probably the only person in the neighborhood, perhaps in the whole town, not too busy to spend these moments in union and adoration. Hundreds of others are serving God, having offered their good works for His glory, but I have leisure for the quiet prayer of praise and thanksgiving. My prayer of thanksgiving should be as spontaneously natural as was the tenth leper's return to Christ, Who had healed him, for God has given me the ability to be articulate. Our Lord does not need words, but never, it seems to me, did He show Himself more like the rest of us than when He expressed His delight in the one leper who did not fail to thank Him as the nine did. Whenever I am pleased by a word of thanks myself, and wonder if a natural weakness prompts my pleasure, I think, "No. Not weakness. A human trait, and one that Jesus did not scorn to share."

Probably very few of the elderly have confessors of
the proper temperament or experience.

August 9

There seems to be a constellation of the feasts of my old saints during these summer months. Here is St. Jean Vianney, the Curé of Ars, whose gentle, wrinkled face is familiar to me because of the many statues of him in French churches. I think the one that I remember best is in St. Roch in Paris. He lived to be seventy-three, in spite of the fact that he is said to have spent as much as sixteen hours daily in the confessional.

My mind keeps returning to the subject of confession for the old. I suppose the ideal situation would be that of an individual who had a confessor, personally wise and holy, thoroughly cognizant of her background, training, interior life, and age; a confessor sufficiently mature, whose spiritual direction would be towards preparation for death and Heaven. But probably very few of the elderly are ideally situated, or have confessors of the proper temperament or experience. Most, no doubt, must make a virtue of necessity, accept being tolerated as trying bores, speak as briefly as possible, trust to the grace of the Sacrament of Penance, then lean on God and their own experience. "To tell one's sins, make an act of contrition, get absolution and run," as St. Teresa would put it in my words! That has been my habit through life, for I have feared much direction, mindful of St. Francis de Sales' advice in regard to choosing a director. But now I wonder if I have depended too much on my own judgment because I feared the harassment incident to not being thoroughly *en rapport*. Again, I compare Aunt Lucy's solution and my mother's, as different as the two were themselves. It is a highly personal matter, and the important thing to remember is that, no matter how elderly and set in habit one is, the Sacrament of Penance continues essential to the end.

The right to reticence is something to treasure.

August 10

What a pleasant summer this has been! My life of doing is largely behind me. From now on, my active means of serving God is prayer, my passive, gentleness and kindness. No particular seeking for good works, taking things as they come, trying not to be exacting of others, noncommital when I can not commend and am not called on to condemn. Truly the right to reticence is something to treasure.

Maybe there is some connection between idling and longevity.

August 11

Old Ned clipped the high hedge today. He told me that he would never be clipping it again. He is retiring this week. We chatted about the old days, he perched on the ladder, and I standing in the drive. He looks back on them as days of prosperity, with a chauffeur, house man, cook, and laundress to serve. He forgets that he was never part of the household, although doubtless he was the recipient of some of the good things that abounded. Ned was thought "no count" in those days. But the years disciplined him to a measure of industry and me to a modicum of patience, and it was with some sadness that I saw him depart this afternoon. I often said that I would not have him on the place; perhaps I was right about that. But I am glad that things worked out in a compensatory fashion, and that he could earn something here when the years overtook him. All the others are dead long ago. Maybe there is some connection between idling and longevity (if one is not a saint). I have always suspected that there might be!

I commend my soul to His care not only at the hour of death, when I leap from life into eternity, but also from hour to hour, from day to day.

August 12

I get comfort from the many Gospel quotations of Jesus' references to His Father. "Father, into Thy hands I commend my spirit." Like Jesus, I surrender my spirit into my Father's keeping. I think that I have come of late to a new understanding of my personal relationship with God the Father. To Him, I am still a child, and He turns to me with paternal love and wisdom. I commend my soul to His care not only at the hour of death, when I leap from life into eternity, but also from hour to hour, from day to day. The older I grow, the more helpless I see myself.

More and more, I think of the fundamental likenesses that make the whole world kin.

August 13

With the development of human sympathy, each individual with whom we come in contact, no matter how casually, seems truly our neighbor. The warmth of heart that the recognition creates is one of the greatest joys of

mature life, and is responsible for much of the merry companionship evident when no thought of social position or
intellectual attainment intervenes. St. John, in old age,
could think of no better advice than, "Little children, love
one another." The years, throwing all things into true perspective, show how silly is worldly snobbishness. I think
there are few any more class-conscious than I, or readier
to concede that birth, education, and environment give
common outlooks to the similarly conditioned; it seems
evident to me that most individuals are happiest when
with their own kind. But, more and more, I think of the
fundamental likenesses that make the whole world kin.

*To tell all the truth in written words is to make
ourselves tremulous witnesses to God's power and
our frailty.*

Augttst 14

I have been reading a simple account of the uses to
which a parish priest attempted to put the hours of his
ordinary days. Temptations to procrastinate, to shun the
disagreeable, the petty annoyances of a pastor unprotected by a community, are here set forth clearly and
honestly. It seems to me the ultimate in humility to write
thus of one's littleness, and I have been thinking that
much of the consolation that we derive from the autobiographies of the saints lies in their self-revelation in
homely matters such as these. The great St. Teresa
watching the hour-glass during meditation, and St.
Therese of Lisieux disturbed by the clicking of a neighbor's rosary seem close to us. The confessor who advises

a penitent to sit down and write out with perfect honesty all that has gone to the making of some difficulty or the acquisition of some consolation, knows that a soul thus revealed to its owner is duly humbled. Newman used to say that he liked to meditate pen in hand, and the habit of making the particular examen with pencil and paper is dear to some holy persons. Of course, it is largely a matter of temperament, but to tell all the truth in writ ten words is to make ourselves tremulous witnesses to God's power and our frailty.

The Mother of Christ experienced the beginnings of old age.

August 15

If, as is supposed, our Lady was about sixteen years old when Jesus was born, she was almost fifty at the time of the Crucifixion. And according to tradition, she lived on in St. John's care for some years afterwards. So the Mother of Christ experienced the beginnings of old age. How gladly she must have welcomed the Angel of Death! True to God, in perfect grace, always mindful of the indwelling of the Holy Spirit, she knew as none other could that there awaited her in Heaven the vision of Him Who had chosen her. Today, the feast of her Assumption, I have kept saying to myself Father Tabb's quatrain:

> Nor Bethlehem, nor Nazareth,
>   Apart from Mary's care;
> Nor Heaven itself a home for Him,
>   Were not His Mother there.

August 16

I have often observed the joyous simplicity of nuns too old to teach. Those who once seemed to me bundles of nervous ambition, almost disedifying in their restive effort, now manifest their true vocation to the religious life. I used to think when I was twenty that all religious should retire and pray at sixty. I have not changed my mind.

A well-developed imagination is a great asset in old age.

August 17

A well-developed imagination is a great asset in old age. So much of the enjoyment of the elderly is due to an ability to put themselves in others' places, picturing their lives, their surroundings, accomplishments. I like to listen to a man or woman telling of a grandson's success in working with radar, atomic energy or some entirely new technique, or to hear their descriptions of strange lands as they see them through the eyes of their descendants. All comes to me flooded by the light of sympathy, pointed up by pride. A wonderful warm human interest exists that would not be possible without a cultivated imagination.

Others die, move, forget; circumstances change.
Nothing persists in permanent association save
God and the soul.

August 18

This is one of those clear green and gold days, every leaf visible, with lovely clouds, "French clouds" I always call them to myself, for they remind me of those that hung over the rolling hill studded with white crosses, near Fère-en-Tardenois in the Marne country. Death came close to me when I was so young, perhaps that is why I think of the radiance of days associated with it, and why a peculiarly brilliant day such as this brings back the thought of those I loved. After all, each of them would be glad to know that fields bright in the sunlight were connected with them in my memory. At Mass, I was overwhelmed by the thought of God's continuing presence throughout a whole life. Others die, move, forget; circumstances change. Nothing persists in permanent association save God and the soul. Thinking back, there is no continuity for me save in myself as being and God as being with me. As the years pass, and loneliness increases, it is comforting to remember our Lord's promise, ". . . and I am with you all days unto the consummation of the world." And He is the only one who is!

August 19

I think it is because the French are so logical and because their language lends itself to shades of thought, that their writers on the interior life have had so profound an influence on the devout of other nations. It is

not unusual to note how, when a French author quotes
an English waiter, using translations, there is a sort of
pointing up that clarifies the meaning of the original.
Even Newman, master of prose that he was, does not
suffer when rendered into French, and Faber is more
convincing. That the great Thomas Aquinas, Italian by
birth and upbringing, should have taught in Paris and so,
to a certain extent, passed through the French alembic,
is something to be thankful for. And I think of others,
the French Anselm, who lived in England, and for whose
simple wording of a great truth I am so thankful.

*When others are attentive to me in ways that are
not to my taste but that indicate their generosity, it
is incumbent on me to receive their expressions
cordially.*

August 20

When others are attentive to me in ways that are not
to my taste but that indicate their generosity, it is incumbent on me to receive their expressions cordially. Strangers are often kind to the elderly, and I hope never to
rebuff their courtesy. Especially the advances of little
children, no matter how much time they consume, I shall
try to meet halfway, thus building up in them a delight
in good works.

I am so tired of temptations!

August 21

I am so tired of temptations! I suppose that everyone who reaches my age is. And I know that I shall never be rid of them until the particular judgment. I might be very smug and complacent without the everlasting reminder of my genius for wrong. I have been saying to myself again and again St. Francis de Sales' lines about meekness to ourselves: "Raise up your heart, then, again whenever it falls, but fairly and softly: humbling yourself before God, through the knowledge of your own misery, but without being surprised by your fall; for it is no wonder that weakness should be weak, or misery wretched."

St. Francis' writings were intended for persons in circumstances kin to my own. The ladies of the Visitation lived in the world before going into the convent. St. Jeanne de Chantal, whom St. Francis chose to head the group directed by him, was a chatelaine and a widow. It is curious that the Visitation should have become an enclosed order, so different from the one that he had in mind. Yet, perhaps his spirit was best preserved cloistered; there is a delicacy in it that the rough world might well have coarsened. Modern orders with modern rules were more in line with his scheme for St. Jeanne Françoise, but society was not yet ready.

August 22

Speaking of temptations, I struggled with one not to go to a funeral today, but in the end, went. From now on, with no immediate family to conserve my energy for, I must try to spend myself as our Lord would have me do in human acts of kindness. And where there is a question as to whether or not it is best to express sympathy or do something neighborly, remember that, even if I am rebuffed, to do so is to act as a Christian. The truth is that throughout my life, when I have obeyed the impulse to a kindness, even an unconventional one, the response has been as to something inspired, for I have met with such eager gratitude. My youthful experience of sorrow and pain gave me a quick eye for others' difficulties. There can be no question of convenience in time or place when we rally to others in emergency, and the fatigue that follows on sacrifice of immediate personal plans is very real. However, the very deliberateness of the sacrifice is pleasing to our Lord. Certainly He not only helped when asked, but volunteered.

I know that I had more careful training
than most Catholic children receive, yet I am
sure that grace as a positive quality was not
sufficiently impressed on me.

August 23

Sinlessness was the prerequisite chosen of God for Mary. "Hail Mary, full of grace, the Lord is with thee." Without sin, with God, the Angel Gabriel stressed at the Annunciation.

I know that I had more careful training than most Catholic children receive, yet I am sure that grace as a positive quality was not sufficiently impressed on me. It is right to train children to avoid sin, to preserve baptismal innocence, and it is tragic to think of grace as something lost, even temporarily; but it seems to me that the right approach in teaching is the positive one: grace is something that need not be lost, that having, we have God with us: not God distant, but God present, intimate, ours. The old age of many would be far happier, I am sure, if they had been educated to a true appraisal of sanctifying grace. There would be fewer regrets, and in addition, there would be more understanding of the indwelling of the Holy Spirit.

In His will is our peace.

August 24

Our Lord wishes peace in all its aspects for us. And the thought of His willingness for me to have it comforts me in my loneliness. "Mary!" "Rabboni, Master!" The greeting has sufficed for today's meditation and yesterday's. Quiet in soul, free to adore, Pia's lines in the *Purgatorio* recur to me: "In His will is our peace." The things that are to my peace are the only ones that I plan to seek, no matter what the cost in money and sacrifice, for I can endure privation if I must in order to avoid contention that disturbs the soul and separates the mind from rest in God's presence. Naturally I am not thinking of shrinking from any struggles that God's service demands, such as speaking out for the right when necessary; I refer rather to times when it is permissible to withdraw from any possibility of conflict.

The time has not come for him to be on his knees praying rather than on his feet addressing a committee; but it has come for me.

August 25

Dan telephoned last night, and I am still under the spell of the conversation. For some time, I have seen rocks ahead in their course, and have been praying the Holy Spirit to guide them. My part, and that of others unable to fight for the right, is to pray for wisdom for all those engaged in social endeavor. Peaceful prayer seems very peaceful to one who was ever a fighter when there was a true cause to support, who argued and listened to wrangling over ways and means. But it seems to me that there is no cowardice in my electing prayer as my office in this instance. Dan is strong, intelligent, in touch with the events of the day. The time has not come for him to be on his knees praying rather than on his feet addressing a committee; but it has come for me. That I revel a little in my freedom from responsibility to do anything but listen and pray in this issue, I admit. But God knows that I joined battle eagerly enough when I was worth anything.

So much of our dilemma in organized charity . . . results, I think, from the lack of personal contact with the individuals whom the well-meaning wish to serve.

August 26

St. John reminds us: "Fear is not in charity. Perfect charity casteth out fear." Persons in whom I observe great charity seem to think little about the world's opinion, and to have unbounded courage for God's service; loving God entirely for Himself, they do bravely what His love dictates. So much of our dilemma in organized charity as well as in political life in this country results, I think, from the lack of personal contact with the individuals whom the well-meaning wish to serve. I have always understood the dreamer's longing for a simple society where the approach is direct. How Christian simplicity can be restored to Christian life, I do not know. The habit of fending off by means of assistants and secretaries who prevent the actual meeting of executive and client is responsible, it seems to me, for much of the distrust and confusion evident in modern society. I pray that our clergy, especially, follow the Holy Father's example and remember the worth of being available themselves: praying thus, I ask, I know, for the spirit of sacrifice to the point of exhaustion, perhaps of death; but "unless the grain of wheat falling into the ground die, itself remaineth alone." No delegates are likely to have a cause sufficiently at heart to die for it, yet we go on appointing committees to study, when a few brief talks would make the parties known to each other as human beings at least. My what a long entry! Brought on largely by listening to Dan's telephone talk. A direct approach is what is needed there, and he is shirking it.

August 27

Human powers weary of petition, but God does not. I imagine that our petitions for those in need are a great delight to Him Who promised an answer to our asking.

I pause sometimes and think that our Lord could say to me as He did to St. Philip, ". . . have I been with you so long a time and have you not known me?" I have had so many years now in which to learn to love and understand, and yet, how dull and cold I am.

I think of [St. Augustine] as the erring lad who his mother, St. Monica, considered the son of her tears.

August 28

This is St. Augustine's feast day. I think of him not as the great Doctor of the Church that he was, nor as the author of *The City of God* and *The Confessions,* but rather as the erring lad whom his mother, St. Monica, considered the son of her tears. Monica knew what it was to suffer and pray for conversion and to have her prayers answered. Whenever I read the familiar passage in *The Confessions* in which St. Augustine described his conversation with her when sitting in the window at Ostia while they were recruiting for the voyage to Africa, I am overwhelmed at the thought of Monica's joy. Augustine was rapt in contemplation of Heaven, but was she also rapt, as he thought? Was she not merely thanking God, with a mother's heart, that this had come to pass?

I find some of my contemporaries irksome because their appearance is no longer attractive, and their conversation repetitious.

August 29

I have been admitting to myself that I find some of my contemporaries irksome because their appearance is no longer attractive, and their conversation repetitious; indeed, many of them are exceedingly uninteresting. Now, I must love them entirely for God's sake; they are His friends with whom He abides. I try to adore Him present with them and to remember that He does not find them boring, any more than He does me! Maybe He will give me tolerance and patience and renew my delight in their company. It is not that I forget that they find me less original than formerly; perhaps the very fact that I know that they do makes them seem less desirable. How nice it would be to be entirely simple in a spiritual sense, to do everything with no intention save to please God! I look for entertainment in association quite as if that were its end.

I have one predilection in common with St. Rose, a pleasure in gardening.

August 30

Whenever I write this date, I think of reading that the first Mass ever offered on Mount Mitchell, one of the highest peaks east of the Rocky Mountains, was on the feast of St. Rose of Lima, the first canonized saint of our Western hemisphere, and the Patroness of the Americas.

I have one predilection in common with St. Rose, a pleasure in gardening. When she was a little girl, according to the legend, she threw roses into the air and they fell to earth in the form of a cross. Later, she seemed to endeavor to hide all suffering beneath a mantle of beauty. That is the very epitome of generosity, I think, and one advocated by our Lord when He spoke of voluntary penance.

After a lifetime among sophisticated people, I am not now surprised by much in myself or others.

August 31

I crave to love personal perfection entirely for God's sake, because He desires holiness for me. I am sure that longing for orderliness in the spiritual life may be largely for personal satisfaction, and that, when this is so, an insidious pride agitates. If I aim to avoid sin and to practise virtue purely for God's pleasure in my accomplishment, I can put my reactions to my weaknesses away from me, be sorry for my faults, and not surprised by my failures.

I note in myself less distress when reminded of my faults than I had when I was young. I used to be surprised that they were so evident to others, no matter how evident they were to me, and a sense of disappointment was joined to my misery. Naturally, after a lifetime among sophisticated people, I am not now surprised by much in myself or others, and certainly I have no cause to think that my shortcomings are not readily apparent. I remember being advised in confession in Rome years ago to make a definite act of thanksgiving every time I was told of a fault. I later learned that the priest was considered a great spiritual director. As we grow older and are nearer Heaven, we have a great desire for perfection, and few offer us any positive help towards acquiring it: we have to sense disapproval rather than hear it expressed. I, for one, now welcome any corrections, even some I think unmerited.

New blossoms daily, new hope!

September 1

Every fair morning now, I look out on a wall covered with Heavenly Blue morning-glories, and say a prayer for the store proprietor who gave me the seeds and for a little old woman who made me a present of a banana a few moments later. I was not conscious of any need of pampering when I went into the seed shop to purchase Black Leaf 40 with which to spray the roses, but, when I happened to mention to the owner, a stranger, that my Heavenly Blue morning-glories, not bought from him, had not thriven, he insisted on bestowing on me a package of his seed. On the way home, I stopped in another shop, and an old Italian woman handed me the banana. I ate the fruit and planted the seed, and smiled over the incidents, and probably would have forgotten them had not the vines grown quickly and burst into such wonderful flower. New blossoms daily, new hope! Aunt Lucy always proclaimed morning-glories her favorite flowers; maybe that was why.

Having Jesus, we have all.

September 2

"... And the bread that I will give is My flesh for the life of the world." Our Lord gives us Himself in Holy Communion. Not for us alone, this gift, but "for the life of the world." We become increasingly sure of this as we age and grow less and less in our own estimation. We, of ourselves, have so little to give, but having Jesus, we have all. United to Him, offering Him to His Father, we adore; then we gather into our prayer the world that He came to save.

Real faith undoubtedly leads us to leave certain matters untampered with, to hold back until God's time is ripe.

September 3

Devotion to Divine Providence is natural in old age. When Cardinal Gibbons was very old, and I very young, I marveled at his frequent references to Divine Providence. But he had watched this country torn by civil strife attain peace, renew its ideals, and become a great power. Possibly he looked back on apparent calamities in some periods of our history and saw them as actually providential, just as he knew contemporaneous trials to be exercises for victory. Real faith undoubtedly leads us to leave certain matters untampered with, to hold back until God's time is ripe. The French expression, *s'adapter au pas de Dieu* has no English equivalent, I think, but it is one that I use almost daily in my own regard in my latter years.

Many a time, I would have enjoyed church music
better with my fingers in my ears.

September 4

The little children sang in the gallery during Mass this morning; their voices were soft and sweet. After Mass, when they were singing a recessional and the church was almost empty, a four-year-old, in clean frock and green head-kerchief, stood in a front pew, her back to the altar, regarded the choir, and then deliberately poked her fingers in both ears and held them there. Whether her musical sense or her envy was dominant, I could not say, but a small chorister descended on her swiftly and taught her manners! Many a time, I would have enjoyed church music better with my fingers in my ears.

Now that I am old enough to revel in children's natural behavior, I often find myself thinking of our Lord's delight in it. If we believe in the Real Presence, we are so conscious of the pleasure that it gives Jesus to have children in the church, that nothing that they do distracts our thoughts from Him. As little St. Therese would say, ours is not the prayer of quiet, but it is prayer just the same.

September 5

Our Lord's knowledge of men and their limited comprehension is marvelously brought out in His simple, effective illustrations. His hearers had seen a sparrow fall: they were capable of noting how small the event. That His omniscient Father notes every sparrow's fall, because He is omniscient, is perfect as illustration.

[St. Joan of Valois'] heroism consisted, it seems to me, in upholding the indissolubility of marriage.

September 7

Many of the holiest days since my return from abroad have been spent in the Reading Room of the Public Library. I have been fascinated by the story of Jeanne de France, or, as the English call her, Joan of Valois, the daughter of King Louis XI.

Once the huge tomes that contain her story are on the table in front of me, I forget the coming and going of students, the rustle of pages, the everlasting murmur of the city outside. Of course, the French have long believed that Jeanne was holy; indeed, they thought her so good that they forgot that she was not beautiful also, and when I was in Paris in May, I found some charming representations of her, notably the delicate small statue of her on the facade of the Royal Church of Saint Germain l'Auxerrois. But her father and the young duke to whom he affianced her in babyhood never forgot her crooked back, her lameness, her pockmarked face. Long before she was publicly repudiated by her husband after he became King Louis XII of France, and her marriage annulled, she had known neglect and sorrow enough to defeat a less courageous woman. I have been reading the old chronicles, those of Commines, Guillaume de Villeneuve, and Jean Bouchet, and Maulde-la-Clavière's edition of the *Procès du divorce de Louis XII* in his volume, *Procédures politiques du règne de Louis XII.* Jeanne's dignity and her soft deep voice made a tremendous impression when she appeared for trial in the Cathedral of St. Gatien in Tours. As I read, knowing, of course, the fate of Princess Jeanne, who considered herself the true wife of Louis XII and the rightful Queen of France, I kept thinking of the other Jeanne, the Maid of Orleans, who set out from this very church to battle for the Princess' grandfather and have him crowned king at Reims.

Well, I can number both among my saints who have suffered most, though neither among my old saints. Jeanne de Valois' marriage was, as was almost a foregone conclusion, declared null and void. As Duchess of Berry, she retired to Bourges, and there founded the Order of the Annonciades before she died at the age of forty. I had not been struck by the fact that both Jeannes will have been canonized during my own lifetime until I wrote the above lines. But I had not forgotten that Jeanne de Valois' final canonization comes about in a century in which divorce is all too prevalent. Her heroism consisted, it seems to me, in upholding the indissolubility of marriage. She was sure that no impediment existed, and although she must have dreaded the ordeal, she defended her rights, even pleading in her clear voice that no advantage be taken of her ignorance: "My lords, I am but a woman, and unacquainted with lawsuits. . . ."

The trials of both Jeannes, both recorded as they proceeded, have enthralled me at different times. At the moment, I am completely under the spell of this gentle woman whom the French called the Cinderella of the Valois.

I shall forever rejoice in the thought of the hours
that I spent last spring in Rome watching merry
games in the streets and parks.

September 8

I note in myself a quality evident in my mother in the
last days of her life, an intensified delight in the joy displayed by little children. She would permit a child to
play with anything that would not injure him—a watch,
a trinket, a lock and key, my typewriter—with a happiness almost as irresponsible as his. With the passing
years, our sense of values is keener, and we realize the
importance of delight. I shall forever rejoice in the
thought of the hours that I spent last spring in Rome
watching merry games in the streets and parks. The children jumping rope in the Borghese Gardens or hunting
bottle caps near Tasso's Oak on the Janiculum, or play-
ing with chalk on the steps of the Chiesa Nuova, gave
me far more pleasure than all the statuary in the Vatican
Gallery.

A saint would be of little help to his contemporaries
if he spoke in a manner different from theirs.

September 9

I was considering the old saints this afternoon when I
was sitting on the porch too tired to do anything, and it
occurred to me that St. Paul of the Cross, the founder of
the Passionists, was in his eighty-second year when he
died. I had known little about him, when one bright
winter day many years ago, I was with some other

young people on the Cælian Hill. We were hiking along merrily when someone suggested that we go into the church of Sts. John and Paul. I remember nothing whatsoever about the church, but I do recall being somehow caught up in a group of visitors and being literally forced to the altar beneath which St. Paul of the Cross' body lay.

I suspect that this great founder has not been particularly fortunate in his biographers. About this, however, I may be mistaken. He was of the Italy of the eighteenth century as St. Therese of Lisieux was of the France of the nineteenth, and there are certain aspects of both periods that are out of accord with our modern ideas. I think that we have to recall that the rococo and Victorian manners of writing and speaking affected the letters and addresses of the saints. Some were extravagant, others stilted. Even the writings of St. Francis de Sales, one of the moulders of the French language and the Patron of Catholic Writers, are full of sixteenth-century conceits. Taken all in all, a saint would be of little help to his contemporaries if he spoke in a manner different from theirs. I know that it is not fair to lay anything sugary in the Little Flower's verse at the door of Queen Victoria, but what I am trying to say is that St. Paul of the Cross and St. Therese of Lisieux wrote and were written of in a style that to us is out of date rather than quaint, whereas St. Francis of Assisi's idiom is ancient enough to fascinate.

By the time we reach real old age, we have little obligation to form others' characters.

September 11

Doubtless there are occasions when we elderly have the right to the harder portion. One morning at Mass, our old pastor rose and commented on the crowded state of the church at the late services, then suggested that the older members of the congregation, already inured to difficulty, be the early risers, attend the first Masses, and leave space for the young at the late. This holds in many contingencies, perhaps, the deliberate choice of the penitential way as a charity to others. I know that it can be overdone in a household and cause some members to grow up in selfishness, but by the time we reach real old age, we have little obligation to form others' characters: rather, I think we have a duty to effect peace and concord even if we seem to be overindulgent.

September 12

It must be wonderful to have a devotion so evident that our friends link us with it, a devotion to the Trinity, the Blessed Sacrament, our Lady. Nobody who knew Father Price, the Tarheel Apostle and the co-founder of Maryknoll, can think of him without remembering his devotion to the Blessed Virgin. The other day, I came across a copy of Father Tabb's poems that he had given to Aunt Lucy, and realized what he and the blind poet whom he knew at St. Charles' had in common: a filial intimacy with Mary.

This is the anniversary of his death, at fifty-nine, in

Hong Kong, and the feast of the Holy Name of Mary. The little book is all that I have left that ever belonged to him, for I gave away the medal blessed by Pope Pius X that he brought me from Rome.

September 13

One delightful freedom that I enjoy these days is the right to commend without seeming fulsome or insincere. Our Lord acknowledged goodness and effort, spoke the word of praise, sent ordinary men and women on their way rejoicing. When we encourage honestly, we imitate Him.

Days, which seemed endless in youth, pass almost unnoticed as middle-age wanes. Nights, too.

September 14

It is a blessing that in most lives, the season of intense loneliness comes late rather than early. Days, which seemed endless in youth, pass almost unnoticed as middle-age wanes. Nights, too. By now, we have the habit of prayer, the recollection of God's presence, the ability to turn to our Lord as an understanding companion.

*None of us grows old without experience of
vicarious suffering.*

September 15

When I watch those whom I love suffer, I ask our
Lady's help. Undoubtedly her greatest pain was vicarious,
for Jesus. She knew His capacity for suffering, how His
love for His persecutors heightened His sorrow when
they lashed Him, how hurt He was by His disciples'
denial and desertion. And to her share in the pain of Jesus
was added her own sadness.

None of us grows old without experience of vicarious
suffering, for our sympathies develop with the years.
Part of the difficulty in accepting pain for those whom
we love is that we are not always certain how they
accept it. In Rachel's case, I must rely on my knowledge
of human nature; a person whom I trust in other ways, I
trust here. I think there are few in the world without the
capacity for true heroism; certainly, I always marvel at
the bravery with which most persons endure trial.

*It requires greater patience to bear suffering that
does not provoke spoken sympathy.*

September 17

St. Francis of Assisi bore in his body the stigmata. All
who saw him saw the wounds in his hands and side and
feet. When St. Catherine of Siena was stigmatized, she
asked God that the pain remain, but the marks be invisible. Catherine had spent much of her life among the
sick, nursing the incurable, the plague-stricken, and she

must have realized that it requires greater patience to bear suffering that does not provoke spoken sympathy. The hardship of which only God and we are mindful, chronic pain of long standing that wearies, and to which others are accustomed and forget that we endure, becomes a secret, passive penance.

Whenever I am tempted to complacency, I am struck down by something untoward, some awkward happening or physical disability.

September 18

I have been thinking of the very old Sister Sacristan at our convent school, Sister Dismas. She spoke broken English, and we liked to ask her who her saint was and hear her reply, "I am the Good Thief." Then she would move off slowly to light the altar candles. I was too young to appreciate the excellence of Dismas as a patron for the aged, but she, who lived close to our Lord, knew. "Amen I say to thee, this day thou shalt be with me in paradise."

The thought of suffering and humiliation is natural this week, with the September Ember Days, the feasts of the Exaltation of the Holy Cross, the Seven Dolors, and the Stigmata of St. Francis at hand. I seldom humble myself voluntarily, nor do I seek a hard and painful course, but I do try to thank God for bringing me to earth so consistently and persistently that, whenever I am tempted to complacency, I am struck down by something untoward, some awkward happening or physical disability.

*Child of God and heir of Heaven, and Heaven not
too far off, he has a right to laughter.*

September 19

I read *Richard II* last night, probably because the print
is good. Shakespeare's aged characters amaze me in their
rightness. Here we find York saying, "Things past
redress are now with me past care." I have often thought
that an elderly person who rejoiced in irresponsibility,
who delighted in the fact that his days of great decisions
were over and he himself free to meet life with childlike
gaiety, was a boon. Frequently there is in an old man's
mirth the quality that a saint's mirth has. Child of God
and heir of Heaven, and Heaven not too far off, he has
a right to laughter. Today my mind has harked back to
my eighty-year-old patient in the cancer ward. When I
would enter at eight in the morning, he would be lying
in bed, shaved, his prayers said, and a long day ahead to
spend with anyone amusing, from Zuleika Dobson to
Doctor Johnson. Sometimes he would be chuckling over
Reeves, sometimes touring the Hebrides with a volume
of Boswell borrowed from me. One morning, he was
reading with perfect absorption, and I remarked on his
delight in the book of the moment. He confided, "It fas-
cinates me. I knew so many of the persons mentioned in
it; it is Maisie Ward's *Gilbert Keith Chesterton.*" Then,
startled by the realization that the assertion would place
him for me, he asked me not to reveal his background of
Downside and an English university. I assured him that I
would not, entirely unnecessarily, for nobody among the
superannuated truckmen and longshoremen in our ward
knew Chesterton from Adam. The little slip of the
tongue was responsible for happy moments for him and

for me. When I could steal time from less congenial occupations, I would listen to his accounts of his youth. I never asked him what misfortune had brought him to a charity hospital for incurables, and he never volunteered the information. But, with a tenderness born of true sympathy he taught me how to enjoy being alone. We shared an interest in books and gardening, and he would give me a battered volume or suggest treatment for my white lilac that was ailing that summer. When at last, he lay still, his heavy black rosary wrapped around his wrist, he would rouse himself and inquire, "How are you, my dear?" And I would leave his alcove trying to check the tears. I owe to the chance friendship more than my frequent recitation of the *De Profundis* for him will ever repay. To be merry at eight in the morning may be relatively easy if one knows the nature of one's malady as he did: there could not be many more mornings before he would be saying Lauds in Heaven.

September 22

Perhaps kindness is the most selfless of all virtues. To me, it seems one of the most admirable. Usually, I can express my gratitude for a kind act only in instant thanks and then in prayer. Often I pray for a saleswoman or a messenger boy or mechanic, or for a stranger who has given me a street direction, asking God to reward all for their goodness to me.

*I am glad now that the young expect their
presence to give me pleasure.*

September 23

It comes with something of a shock to realize that I
have little to add to anyone's merriment, that I am at the
age to be borne with, suffered! I remember a very old
American lady who spent a summer in a hotel with us in
Switzerland. She would come into the card room and ask
gently if we objected to her watching our game. What
glee she would get from a finesse or grand slam, especially if my mother were the successful player! Her
approbation doubled the value of a trick. I enjoyed having her present. I am glad now that the young expect
their presence to give me pleasure. Little children are
exacting, of course, but there is a marvelous generosity
evident in the teen-age group.

September 25

I have been watching a kind man directing some
laborers. I like to think of all love as a radiation of God's
love, so that the gentle dealings of human beings seem
always an expression of Him.

There would be the fragrance of pine and juniper warm in the sun, and the glory of thousands of trees turning saffron along the shores.

September 26

It is not surprising that I think of St. Isaac Jogues this bright autumn day, his feast. How I did love his lake in September when, the summer visitors gone, there was hardly a sound to be heard except the ripple of waves against the canoe and their gentle plash on the rocky islands! There would be the fragrance of pine and juniper warm in the sun, and the glory of thousands of trees turning saffron along the shores. But, always, the brilliant sparkle of the water entranced me most, water so clear that Jogues called the lake after the Blessed Sacrament. The tragedy of the mutilation of his hands that had been anointed to consecrate seems doubly great when I think of his devotion to the Holy Eucharist. But he journeyed back to France, obtained permission from Rome to celebrate Mass again, and then returned to sacrifice his whole body for his beloved Indians. He was but thirty-nine when martyred, but old in the experience of torture. I love his France and his lake, and he is one of my saints.

Today we laughed over the memories that nobody shares with us.

September 27

Taking Mollie and her three-year-old daughter with me, I drove out to the sanatorium to see Mrs. Lane. She is over eighty now, white-haired, clear-skinned, erect, and very devout. The Sisters entertained the little girl, giving her milk and cookies and listening to her prattle, and, while Mollie chatted with a friend of her own, I was free to enjoy Mrs. Lane. I wonder if the few of my mother's old friends who are left realize how much I delight in their company. Today we laughed over the memories that nobody shares with us. When I am with Mrs. Lane or Mr. Ware, I renew my youth. They thank me for my calls. But I am the beneficiary.

Whenever you behold the glories of this world, lift up your heart and begin to be now what you intend to be then.

September 30

Another constellation of feasts of the old, St. Jerome's today. Domenichino's painting, *The Last Communion of St. Jerome*, is so familiar that nobody forgets him portrayed as aged. That picture horrified me when I used to see it in the Vatican when I was a girl, and since, I have tried to think of the great Doctor of the Church without its coming to mind. It is true that St. Jerome grew old. But he loved the young. Last spring when I was at San Girolamo della Carità, the church built on the site of the house of his friend Paula, I recalled the letter of condolence that he wrote to Paula's little daughter Eustochium. He besought her to think of her future welcome to Heaven by our Lady and her own saintly mother, and counseled, "Whenever you behold the glories of this world, lift up your heart and begin to be now what you intend to be then." It seems to me that I am forever making just such beginnings. Will I ever get beyond beginning? I suppose that others my age ask themselves the same question.

October 1

I have always been glad that our Lord praised the tenth leper, the one who went back to Him when the nine went their way.

October 3

One of the most remarkable things about St. Therese of Lisieux is the fact that she recognized the value of the "little way" when she was very young. Young people usually see themselves doing great things, leading lives of heroism. It is the experienced who see their own unimportance, and are content to serve God in a humble fashion. It is pleasant as I grow older to think of myself as a child in God's household and to remember the value of small acts. The child who picks up threads when her mother has been sewing, or hands her small articles when asked for them, does not fret because she is not of greater assistance, but rejoices in her own minute part. I have every reason to know myself incapable of much effort, but I do like to realize that God occasionally uses my willingness for His ends.

The desire to learn to love increases.

October 4

The desire to learn for learning's sake and for the worldly uses to which knowledge may be put, undoubtedly diminishes with the years. But the desire to learn to love increases. I copied recently lines on the act of charity in Monsignor Prunel's *La Grace:* " . . . the intelligence, knowing God supernaturally, understands that He is the sovereign good, worthy of a sovereign love. . . ."

I have been handling volumes associated with different members of the family, dipping into one after another, reading a paragraph here and there.

October 5

We cleaned books today. Because Joel has done such work at the library for many years, I can trust him with most of it. He knows the Roman numerals, and does not come to me to help him place "Volume Ex Two Eyes" as Ezra always did. I have been handling volumes associated with different members of the family, dipping into one after another, reading a paragraph here and there, remarking that many of Aunt Lucy's books were boldly marked, my mother's rarely annotated. I came across some lines written by Aunt Lucy on the fly-page of my grandmother's fine copy of *Paradise Lost;* she probably chose that because she knew it to be a book that her sisters would cherish because their mother's. The note was dated 1882. Aunt Lucy was twenty-four years old at the time. She recorded the fact that she had had such severe pain that she apprehended death. In the event of its coming suddenly, she, the oldest of the group of Catholic girls, wanted them to know that she was prepared. The attacks proved to be *angina pectoris,* a true angina, and were the first of a series. Yet, she outlived her younger sisters and died of cancer in the room in which I am writing, sixty-four years after penning that message.

October 6

Today I was teaching Rachel, almost blind since babyhood and now entirely so, and a Protestant, of course, to say the Rosary. When I took her hands to let her feel the divisions of the beads into decades, she lingered over the crucifix, fingering the cross and the çorpus. She confided that she had never known that a crucifix was a cross with a corpus attached. It was an infinitely moving experience, and as she learned the Hail Mary and the decades of the Joyful, Sorrowful, and Glorious Mysteries, pausing to comment on the fact that our Lord's life was here in miniature, I realized that it was easier to get non-Catholics to appreciate the Rosary than I had anticipated, for their grounding in the New Testament prepares them for the prayers and meditations largely of Gospel origin.

*The Rosary is well fitted to the capacity of the
afflicted. No need to hear, or see, or speak.*

October 7

The Blessed Virgin must take particular delight in
the Rosaries of the old. The Rosary is well fitted to the
capacity of the afflicted. No need to hear, or see, or
speak. I have stood often in a cancer ward and watched
the beads slip through thin, gnarled fingers. "I try to be
good," a wasted old gardener or sailor would tell me, a
twinkle in his eye, "I said a Rosary for you." These old
charity patients pray as the great Newman prayed in his
armchair when he could no longer read his breviary.

*It takes a great measure of trust and abandonment
to face dependence on others.*

October 8

I have been struggling with temptations to solicitude.
In so far as material things are concerned, it takes a
great measure of trust and abandonment to face dependence on others. Physical and financial dependence is
the lot of the majority of the old people in this country.
I think of myself as blessed in that I do not anticipate
lack of means to pay for my care, but, should I be
dependent on charity, I could but beg God for a holy
acceptance of my helplessness. He could give even wil-
ful me a determination to wrest to His glory and my
soul's salvation hardships incident to age, teaching me
finally the true meaning of *Fiat voluntas tua.*

I hope that I shall never be too old
to enjoy baseball.

October 9

The Yankees won the World Series today. We cleaned
books all week, so I had a reason to be close to the radio.
I hope that I shall never be too old to enjoy baseball.
When my mother was eighty, and both radios got out of
order the day of a final game, I coaxed a mechanic here
by telling him of her interest in the Series. He mended
one set and sat on the floor beside it listening, while I
relayed the plays with a pencil and paper to my deaf
baseball fan. The Yankees won that day too. It was my
mother's last game, and how she did enjoy it!

October 10

Newman and St. Vincent de Paul, both deeply concerned with the thought of age, grew old. A preoccupation
with the soul's passing was Newman's from middle life,
and I recall various verses and passages of his that mention it, as well as his curious attraction to one of the oldest of saints, Philip Neri. St. Vincent's interest in age was,
of course, natural to one zealous for the alleviation of all
misery. His charities for the senescent were forerunners of
that of Jeanne Jugan, who founded the Little Sisters of the
Poor. With characteristic French logic, Vincent and Jeanne
established homes from which the inmates could take off
for celestial regions. I have been smiling to myself over the
remark made by a Sister of the Good Shepherd to a Little
Sister: "We work with our girls and never know what the
outcome will be. And you give your old people a shove,
and they're safe in Heaven."

*[God] can do in an instant what I have not
accomplished in a lifetime.*

October 11

Our Lord shows Himself the good physician when He tells us that what is in store for us will hurt. "But have confidence," He insists. I need to make many acts of confidence with a special effort to consider God's omnipotence. He can do all things and does not require me to plan too far ahead, but rather desires the total resignation of all my affairs to Him. He can do in an instant what I have not accomplished in a lifetime. I am resolved not to fret about matters, for worry is incompatible with confidence. A saying attributed to St. Philip Neri comes to me: "Cast yourselves with confidence into the arms of God; and be very sure of this, that if He wants anything of you, He will fit you for your work and give you strength to do it." And St. Philip said, also, "Excessive sadness has in general no other root than pride."

*When the weather is bad, I often think of
St. Francis de Sales' straddling an icy plank
in order to cross a stream to reach the chapel.*

October 13

If I had a cloak that would make me invisible, I would put it on whenever I went to daily Mass. Living among non-Catholics, my going is noted, commented on, given as a reason for my occasional fatigue. And seen at Mass day after day in different places, I have picked up the most amazing set of acquaintances. I would hide behind a column in the church in a Swiss resort in vain, for I would be ferreted out by an old lady, deposited in her millionaire son-in-law's fine car and driven by a liveried chauffeur to our hotel. On the ship last spring, I needed the desired invisibility in a special manner, yet, had I possessed it, I would have missed some of the pleasantest chats of the voyage. Walking aft, one afternoon, as we neared the coast of Ireland, I was addressed by an old sailor on deck, "Say a prayer that it will be calm at Glengarriff tomorrow," he said. "That's a terrible place when the wind blows." I thought the requested prayer was for the passengers' comfort until I discovered that Jack was detailed to a landing launch, and that the prayer was for him. He had seen me at Mass.

I was laughing to myself just now at the recollection of being literally forced into driving a stranger's custom built car one morning, she being unable to, and determined not to miss Mass during Lent. When the weather is bad, I often think of St. Francis de Sales' straddling an icy plank in order to cross a stream to reach the chapel. Few who love the Mass fail to discover a means to get to church.

My mother was certain that most persons in the world had about all they could carry.

October 14

I have no excuse for failure in tolerance, for I have sufficient intelligence to understand that my neighbors may have greater temptations and fewer consolations than I imagine. If I can modify my mental judgment through use of my common sense, I will go a long way towards a more charitable approach. My mother was inclined to be severe, but, in late life, she used to paraphrase the saying about knowing and forgiving, converting it to, "To know all is to understand all." Much that we are not called on to forgive because we are not personally involved puzzles us to the point of distress. My mother was certain that most persons in the world had about all they could carry. As I sit back and observe and reason about others' actions, I am convinced that this is true.

All things are passing, God only is changeless.

October 15

The feast of St. Teresa. I do not pray to St. Teresa as often as I do to St. Catherine of Siena, whose direct approach is more comprehensible to me than that of any woman saint save Mary Magdalen. But I owe Teresa much. I think gratefully of her definition of humility, of her insistence that the least unfaithfulness to God was never to be passed over, of her struggles with distractions and weariness in prayer, of her watching the hour-glass, and of her courage in old age. With all her journeys and illnesses, she lived to be older than I am.

"All things are passing, God only is changeless," an elderly Christian repeats with her. The unchanging God, ever loving, ever patient and merciful, without Whose will I would not be: and this self created by Him for Himself. This soul so old in my sight save when He teaches me to regard it as young in His! St. Teresa knew. She was sixty-seven when she died.

October 17

As a rule, I endeavored to please my mother, for I was conscious that her independent nature made of her deafness a particularly great affliction. She often reminded us that it was difficult to live with the deaf, but still more difficult to be deaf. The recollection of our relationship is vivid today. On one occasion I failed her. We were at Vichy together, and she longed to go to Paray-le-Monial because she loved St. Margaret Mary, whose convent had been there. I can not remember the details of the matter. She had a fine disregard for distances and time tables, and these must somehow have entered the picture. Whenever this feast of St. Margaret Mary arrives, my compunction is renewed and draws me to her, for her life was so full of awkwardness and misunderstanding, and her heart so close to the Sacred Heart, that she sympathized with the inept.

Two of the lovely canticles that St. Luke recorded were the utterances of elderly men.

October 18

Were it not for St. Luke's Gospel, we would not have the *Nunc Dimittis* and the *Benedictus* and the accounts of the old people near our Lord in His infancy. Zachary and Elizabeth, Simeon and Anna, and the Doctors in the Temple had thought long about the coming of Christ before they saw Him. Two of the lovely canticles that St. Luke recorded were the utterances of elderly men. In the morning, at Lauds, we say Zachary's *Benedictus*: in the evening, at Compline, Simeon's *Nunc Dimittis.* From

childhood, we love Zachary's verse: "Blessed be the
Lord God of Israel because he hath visited and
wrought the redemption of his people." In the evening
of life, we come to love in a new manner Simeon's
words: "Now thou dost dismiss thy servant, O Lord,
according to thy word in peace."

October 19

Many of my contemporaries are ill or afflicted. When
I am depressed by this, or inclined to be made impatient
by the inconvenience their maladies cause me, I remember that the deaf, the blind, the lame, and those whose
speech was impaired, were especially dear to Jesus. If I
make every effort to recall this, I shall not yield to the
temptation to avoid those who are in the greatest need
of companionship.

October 20

Pity and tenderness and all the concomitants of sympathy are easier virtues to live with than stern justice.
Strictness with others has always exhausted me, and now
that I know that life itself is a mighty disciplinarian, I am
seldom exacting with anyone, young or old.

October 21

The experience of life packed into the psalms calls forth an echo in the mature person. Not didactical (the elderly abhor instructive writing), they are cries of the heart, utterances of the suffering, joyous aged.

October 22

Yesterday, on half-an-hour's notice by telephone, Frank and his four-under-seven arrived. We had a tea party. The baby was on the table part of the time, the others under it at pleasure, although cambric tea was the strongest drink. Little Tony, a ritualist at six, proposed "doing what we did last time," so they went up the front stairs and down the back, again and again, as fast as their fat legs would carry them. The baby crawled in the wake, and Frank trailed the baby. The afternoon was a perfect success for me as well as for their mother; she did not come.

Any of us might well pray, "Jesus, teach me silence."

October 23

My horror of the mischief that careless old people can do in a community increases. Any of us might well pray, "Jesus, teach me silence," and the aged, who have been aware of the good and bad that conditioned the families in a town, should do so. It is easy, in replying to a casual comment, to answer carelessly, taking it for granted that the person with whom we converse is familiar with an old tragedy or scandal. I think that the elderly, by reason of their accumulated knowledge, have a responsibility not altogether unlike that that confessors have. Many aged men and women do harm without suspecting it. Even when their memory is perfect, and it is often amazingly accurate in regard to long-past events, they are not enough in touch with their surroundings to realize the repercussions that an idle bit of gossip might have. For myself, I have infinitely greater peace when I deliberately avoid mention of any human being.

October 24

When the elderly are selfish, the pity of their fault seems very great. Most of life is lived, and we should be willing to yield place, ambitions. Granted that the selfishness of the young is partly accountable for the selfishness of the old, nevertheless, the latter, holding to a minimum with avidity, seem more mistaken.

The galleries [in New York] are a delight, and particularly rich in masterpieces in which old persons are depicted.

October 25

I returned from New York today. The galleries there are a delight, and particularly rich in masterpieces in which old persons are depicted. My mind running on the subject of senescence, I noted these more readily than I ever have. The Altman Collection of Rembrandts in the

Metropolitan contains many fine portraits of the aged, of course. And the amazing etching of the Presentation "in the dark manner" fascinated me again. The Memlings seem to me especially fine; the lined faces in the portraits more interesting than the smooth young beauty that some painters show. Never before had I been so impressed by Quentin Matsy's "Adoration of the Magi"; there, the oldest of the Kings is an old, old man: his thin white hair, his hollow temples indicate this, but something of age over and above the physical was caught in painting the expression of the face. There is a very interesting bust, thought to be that of St. John Fisher by Torrigiano, that I had never seen before; its expression, also, is remarkable for feeling.

I dropped into the Frick Gallery to see Holbein's St. Thomas More and El Greco's St. Jerome. The latter is far more like the St. Jerome of my imagining than the Domenichino masterpiece or any of the numerous pictures featuring the lion of the *Golden Legend*. El Greco painted him as old, dignified, learned; gaunt, of course, for who would not be so after such labors as his on the Vulgate? A nimble youth, on a bright, clear day, could find many an old saint to catalogue on New York's Fifth Avenue.

October 27

I have been thinking of the conversations during our Lord's Hidden Life. His talks with His Blessed Mother were never recorded, but I feel sure that He told her about His mission, His suffering, and His glory, to prepare her for what was ahead.

This has been a bright day, crisp and cool. I raked
sun-warmed oak leaves for an hour or two.

October 28

This has been a bright day, crisp and cool. I raked
sun-warmed oak leaves for an hour or two. Their fragrance reminded me of my childhood. The postman
came while I was in the yard. He brought a marked copy
of the magazine. My account turned out better than I
had expected. I was amazed to be in the company of
such learned writers, but am fortunate in the fact that
my contribution had not been subjected to translation,
whereas theirs had. Few translations from the French
retain the flavor of the original; there are nuances in the
idiom that English does not convey.

The making of little oases of peace is the duty
of the aged.

October 30

I was surprised that the sermon today, the last Sunday
in October, was not on Christ the King. Our young
priests, with their deep and loving belief in the divinity
of Jesus, know little about the time-honored idea of sov-
ereignty, and perhaps it is natural that the feast has not
made the same appeal in this country as abroad. Even in
Europe, of course, the idea of monarchy vanishes fast.
For me, who am old enough to ally reverence and rule,
there is a charm in meditating not only on the thought
that the kingdom of God is within me, but also on Jesus
as King, Ruler of all nations. Hope for universal peace

was in Pope Pius XI's heart when the feast was instituted. One World War had ended. It was not known that
a second would begin. Now, the world is in such turmoil
that I see no possibility of world peace in my lifetime;
but I do believe it worth while to cultivate in each individual a love of personal peace. That the making of little
oases of peace wherever they are is the duty of the aged,
seems more apparent to me every day.

*I wonder if children now are not more natural
than we were. We were friendly and polite, but
nursemaids cramped our style.*

October 31

How air mail simplifies communication! A letter from
Fred's London editor, accepting my sketch, came today.

This is Hallowe'en, and I have just turned off the
porch light, thus announcing to small witches and gob-
lins and all their weird associates that the cookies, kisses,
candies, apples, and other appropriate delicacies have
met their fate, that the larder is empty and the lady of the
house worn to a thread. Hordes of children began arriv-
ing soon after dusk. We go through the same ritual every
year. First, I hear the young voices outdoors. Then the
ring of the doorbell. I go to the front door and find an
array of perfectly silent children in fancy dress. I register
surprise, provide refreshments, and then the fun begins.
I guess and guess and guess the identity of each caller,
and finally, of course, guess right, for the unpardonable
faux pas is to fail to recognize a child. I suppose they
think that their disguises heighten their individuality. As

the years go on, I find it something of a burden to be expected to remember what each boy and girl represented last Hallowe'en. "Oh, don't you remember me?" one little girl wailed, "I was the White Rabbit last year and you said," etc.

I wonder if children now are not more natural than we were. We were friendly and polite, but nursemaids cramped our style. No danger of overtraining by nursery governesses for this generation.

I am sure that there are many saints in Heaven who are entirely surprised to discover that they are saints.

November 1

All Saints' Day, the day of the unrecognized holy, and a favorite feast of mine. I am sure that there are many saints in Heaven who are entirely surprised to discover that they are saints. One day when my mother was sewing, her seamstress volunteered, "Miss Louise is a saint," mentioning a little lame maiden lady of our acquaintance. "How do you know?" my mother asked. And the seamstress replied, "I can't describe it. But I know. There is something about a saint." I doubt if Miss Louise suspected her sanctity, but I do not doubt that she is among those whom we honor today.

Scarcely a week passes now that is not marked by the death of a friend.

November 2

All Souls' Day. Scarcely a week passes now that is not marked by the death of a friend. Wherever I go, memories crowd upon me, and I find myself saying the *De Profundis* as I walk by a house or corner. So, in a way, I live in constant remembrance of the souls in Purgatory, with the psalm that the Church specifies for them forever in my prayers. It is a comforting psalm and there is nothing sad for me in its being a prayer for the dead. When little Aunt Lucy was in the last stages of her malady, she and I would say it together while we waited for the hypodermic to take effect. If I paused purposefully, failing to say my verse, she would right matters until too drowsy to do so. Conditioned by two world wars, and in the midst of a family beset by sudden death, for, as Margaret says, we are "a family of accidents," I have never shunned the thought of my own. Now I ponder it in a manner far from academic. Probably I shall be in a hospital, among strangers or alone, but I cannot see that that matters greatly, for, after all, all my spiritual crises are inevitably concerned with none but God and myself, and my last may well be so. If God wills that I be fortified by the Sacraments, He will so arrange, and the question gives me only ordinary care. To live close to God now is more important than to make elaborate preparations for my end. And with that practical streak that dominates my thinking, I realize how seldom death comes with the dignity we plan. The soul is God's. He can take mine as He pleases.

November 3

Young people are often unthinkingly generous, giving what they have with prodigality. Whereas the elderly, when they give, do so with open eyes. It would take more courage to make the Heroic Act, by which one gives to the Holy Souls all the indulgences gained by one or for one, here or hereafter, at sixty than at sixteen. The reckoning of indulgences gained for the Holy Souls is a more heart-warming occupation than calculation for oneself. And to give all, once and for all, is to imbue with the glow of charity every intention. Probably the Little Flower was right in her surmise regarding mathematics in Heaven. For my part, this phase of arithmetic is one with which I do not concern myself.

I think that intellectuals, forever engaged in study and writing, have less opportunity to pray than the rest of us.

November 4

The weather has been fine, and I have spent many hours out of doors raking leaves and making ready for winter. Living in the oak woods I often think of "Thick as autumnal leaves that strow the brooks in Vallombrosa." I am sure that Vallombrosa's leaves are no thicker than ours! I have planted bulbs. They look so drab, ugly, and unpromising that I can hardly believe them responsible for the brilliant flowers of spring, the crocuses and scilla, the daffodils and tulips and fragrant hyacinths. I glory in the brilliant blue of scilla, so I planted more than usual this year.

A small Catholic came while I was working. I asked her

if she prayed for me. "Yes," she replied instantly. "First, I pray for the whole world. Then for my family and the neighbors, and for you." That prayer for the whole world first indicates the child's intelligence. To include all nations and races is right, then to realize that there are individuals whom we must serve specially in the only way possible to us, by petition to the Father. Working out of doors frees the mind for prayer. I think that intellectuals, forever engaged in study and writing, have less opportunity to pray than the rest of us. Gardening and housework are not too absorbing, and if one can not be a shepherd, the saint-making occupation, these serve very well for the promotion of the contemplative life.

November 9

Today, in the autumn woods, rejoicing in the saffron of the hickory leaves and the wine hues of the oaks, I found myself longing to share their beauty with others. Then I knew that having nobody to enjoy the scene with me, I must refer all nature's works to God, and praise Him in a *Benedicite* of my own.

I spend hours out of doors when the sun shines.

November 10

The autumn foliage has made me remember a verse in Browning's "By the Fire-side." The poem caught my fancy when I was young. Concerned as it is with the time "When the long dark autumn evenings come . . . in life's

November too," and describing an old poet by the hearth, deep in Greek, it had a natural appeal for a girl who loved Italy that "woman country, wooed not wed," to which the bard alludes. I liked the stanza telling of the November hours,

> That crimson the creeper's leaf across
>   Like a splash of blood, intense, abrupt,
>
> O'er a shield else gold from rim to boss,
>   And lay it for show on the fairy-cupped
> Elf-needled mat of moss.

This year the trees seem to vie with each other in brilliance; the maples, hickories, and dogwoods are in their glory. I spend hours out of doors when the sun shines, for, given one heavy rain and a cold west wind, and the radiance of this lovely fall will yield to wintry greyness.

I am truly thankful that I obeyed my impulse and went abroad last spring.

November 12

A strong gust of wind blew a heavy car door onto my leg and broke it, an exceedingly painful accident. I must make the best of matters. There is not much Pollyanna philosophy at my disposal, but I am truly thankful that I obeyed my impulse and went abroad last spring. With nobody to bring books from the library, I shall entertain myself with those in the house. There will be leisure to do something that I have longed to do, that is to read the Bible a book at the time, not interruptedly by chapters, but whole books from end to end.

November 13

I have had many friendly callers, and a plethora of well-meant but uncomprehending advice. I have tried to listen politely, sympathetically, weighing what I heard, ready to yield my will if I decided that my elected course of remaining here was due to stubbornness. I have realized, however, that I have pondered the matter more deeply than anyone. Reasonably sure of my own common sense and the wisdom of my decision, I cannot afford to be tangled in irresolution by those unaware of the intricacies of the problem. During my life, I have found that many times I could carry through with a burden with less mental and physical effort than dropping it and picking it up again would involve.

One of the most disheartening occurrences in any prolonged suffering is distress over one's inability to suffer cheerfully.

November 14

It is easier to bear being laid up now than it was when my being so inconvenienced others. Formerly, it took more self-control to bear being a nuisance than to bear pain. Now, I can take my Rosary in my hand, turn my face to the wall, and know that because I am necessary to nobody's comfort, I can endure in peace. I suppose this is one of the negative assets of aging.

One of the most disheartening occurrences in any prolonged suffering is distress over one's inability to suffer cheerfully. I am old enough to realize that such distress may be due to the malady, for even a slight fever weakens self-control. The humiliation of recognizing one's lack of the spirit of sacrifice is acceptable as prayer, but the seasoned sufferer knows this better than the novice.

November 15

Father Marion very kindly offered to bring me Holy Communion. I have a feeling of kinship with some of the unimportant people in the New Testament: with Peter's wife's mother, for instance, and with Zaccheus, who, low of stature, perched in a sycamore tree the better to see the Master. How astounded he must have been when told that Jesus would go to his house! When Aunt Lucy was very old, yet reluctant to ask that Holy Communion be brought to her, a priest told me to remind her that, when she was able, for years and years, she went to our Lord: now, it was His turn to come to her.

I try, as I get older, to rely more on the knowledge of God's abiding in my soul than on any feeling.

November 16

Some of the sayings of Jesus become dearer and dearer to me as they apply more specifically to the needs of my years: "... and behold, I am with you all days, even unto the consummation of the world"; this assurance of our Lord helps. More and more, He is my only companion, the Friend to Whom I turn during lonely days and nights. Sometimes, I forget His presence, but when I can not manage my vagabond thoughts, He understands. Without the revelations in this regard that Gertrude, Teresa, and Catherine of Siena had, but bolstered by their experience as described in their writings, I try, as I get older, to rely more on the knowledge of God's abiding in my soul than on any feeling. I long to love God with my whole mind, but He knows my mind's limitations, and does not expect perfect recollection of weak me.

I prefer being nurse to patient.

November 18

Endeavoring to accept pain gladly and to remember that suffering is a privilege, I think of the Passion, and especially of the human plea to be spared uttered during the Agony in the Garden. Jesus has not forgotten what He endured, nor is He unmindful of my present state. The trial is not of my choosing, but would I have had the courage to elect anything difficult? Thirty years ago, when reading the letters of St. Catherine of Siena, I was impressed by a passage, ". . . spiritual self-will is not dead in them: therefore they imperiously demand from God that He should give them consolations and tribulations in their own way. . . ." I compare my attitude in illness to that of St. Francis de Sales, who declared himself ready to be sick that his household might have the opportunity to perform a Corporal Work of Mercy. I prefer being nurse to patient. After all, Pascal, who was perhaps not a saint, certainly not a canonized one, wrote the prayer that I may well use now. Parts of it are appropriate: "Give to my heart repentance for my faults, since, without interior sorrow, the sorrows with which my body is afflicted

would be but new occasions of sin. . . ." "Remove from
me, O Lord, the sadness that my self-love might cause me
to suffer at the sight of my own infirmity."

Illness, which renders me physically incapable of
helping myself, teaches me that all I need do is to
exist in God's sight, my will united to His.

November 19

For which thing thrice I besought the Lord that it
might depart from me:

"And He said to me: My grace is sufficient for thee:
for power is made perfect in infirmity. Gladly therefore
will I glory in my infirmities, that the power of Christ
may dwell in me" (II Cor. 12).

When I consider how much of our Christian philosophy
is based on St. Paul's writings, I am thankful that he not
only knew pain but also experienced old age. I frequently find that pain and physical weakness seem to
banish the power to pray. The briefest acts of faith and
love, the recollection that God is present and that His
grace is sufficient, are what I ask of myself. I try to
avoid mental agitation, thinking such almost an insult
to our Lord, Who has chosen this way for me. Illness,
which renders me physically incapable of helping myself,
teaches me that all I need do is to exist in God's sight, my
will united to His; if I can not think, if I can not glory in
my infirmity, I am all the more dependent on His grace.

Reading through the above, I know that such expression might lend itself to my thinking years from now, if I
ever open this notebook, that I believed that the current

accident was planned for me. What I do believe is that there are certain God-given laws in nature, and that these, ordinarily, bring about certain results. . . . God can work a miracle to prevent such results, but, when He does not and we are the victims, it is for us to make prayer of our acceptance. A sudden wind came up, a car door was open, my leg was so placed as to be crushed when it blew to . . . all of that was according to nature. But, this having happened, I must make use of pain. I do not know the exact teachings of the Church on the mystery of pain, but practically speaking, this is all I need.

November 20

Today has been marked by a willing and receptive quiet, an abandonment. I trust, leave all to God. I know that ineffectual effort on my part would be wasteful, destructive.

Growing older, with Heaven nearer, there is a happiness in prayer that it is well to relish to the full.

November 21

Mary, daughter of Joachim and Anna, destined to be the Mother of God, was trained from early childhood for the service of the Lord. Taken to the Temple to learn the practice of prayer, she spent her first youth in preparation for the care she would give Jesus, readying herself, all unknowingly, for continuous, intimate association with the Lord of Lords. At least, that is what I have been thinking on this feast of her Presentation. Not only is Heaven something to prepare for and to anticipate joyfully, but also our seasons of prayer, our communion with God while on earth. And, growing older, with Heaven nearer, there is a happiness in prayer that it is well to relish to the full. I remember being touched by the request of an old cancer patient that his alarm clock be set to waken him early the morning he was going to Holy Communion.

I fear lack of self-control and mischief with temper and tongue because of potential harm to my associates, who cannot allow for irresponsibility as God does.

November 22

I have had a great horror of decrepitude, natural for one who has gloried in independence. But decrepitude is but part of old age, and rightly used, may be valuable. I see no reason why, convinced of God's goodness and mercy, my will in accord with His will, anything should prevent my rejoicing with Him, no matter how old I live to be. As long as I have the use of my mind, I hope to cultivate simplicity, the virtue that directs all my actions to one end, God's pleasure. Then, should my brain be weakened by extreme old age, and I unable to control thought or movement, the lifelong intention will suffice. More than ever then, I shall be God's helpless child.

But I fear lack of self-control and mischief with temper and tongue because of potential harm to my associates,

who cannot allow for irresponsibility as God does . . .
and it is for their sake that I struggle, while competent,
to make kindliness second nature, automatic.

Remember, the whole world is one big city.

November 23

Sitting here in my mother's corner, reading the Bible as
she used to, it came over me that she was in her sixty-
fourth year, older than I am, when at her insistence, we
went to the Holy Land. Aunt Lucy was unwilling to go,
and did not; I was perhaps a little reluctant. Had we not
gone right then, in one of the rare peaceful interludes in
the last four decades, we would never have made the
journey, and I might not be enjoying my present scheme
of reading as I am. I am thankful that Mother had, during the last sixteen years of her life, actual knowledge of
the countryside that she had read so much about and
pictured for so long. As St. Jerome put it in one of his letters, it makes the same difference to an understanding of
Holy Writ to have seen Judea, that it does to an appreciation of the third book of Virgil to have travelled from
the site of Troy via Sicily to the mouth of the Tiber.

To have seen Mount Sion, the Valley of the Jordan, the
site of Jericho, the Plain of Esdraelon, and the blue mountains of Moab adds immeasurably to my delight in reading the Old Testament. As for the New Testament, and the
little "compositions of place" that we are taught to make
when essaying meditation on the life of Jesus, who can
tell! Bethlehem, approached from the Field of the
Shepherds, its domes and arched windows repeating the

curves of the encircling hills: Nazareth, high above the sweeping white roads and undulating plains: lovely Ain Kairim, nestled among the ancient olive trees, probably the place of Mary's *Magnificat,* and the Lake of Genesareth come to my mind often, as does Jacob's Well. The last named is one of the traditional spots to which few if any archaeologists take exception, I believe, for what Jesus said there means more and more to me, and I like to picture Him resting by the well.

My mother was ill many times on that journey. Frequently, I was frightened, for we were travelling without a party, and the care of an elderly deaf person, a stranger in Palestine and Syria, was no sinecure. When we were about to leave Jerusalem for the drive via Damascus to board a ship at Beirut, a giant Franciscan, who called to say good-bye, sensed my anxiety, and advised me, "Remember, the whole world is one big city."

I have learned at least that I am little and weak and sinful, not the person of my youthful imaginings, but beloved of God.

November 24

This is the feast of Saint John of the Cross, St. Teresa's friend and mine. She stated with dismay, when she was trying to plead his cause, that she could find nobody who seemed to remember the poor little man. St. John of the Cross taught the lowliness that brings peace to old people as well as to their families; he knew the value of oblivion, the voluntary oblivion that is a talent with the holy old. Innately proud Teresa, whose faults are so comprehensible to me, was his penitent. She learned much from this small friend of ours, her half-a-friar, and I have learned at least that I am little and weak and sinful, not the person of my youthful imaginings, but beloved of God, a child of His pity.

I am thankful, and I like to tell God that I am.

November 25

Our Lord's "Father, I thank Thee," is a prayer that I want always mine. I am thankful, and I like to tell God that I am.

Yesterday it came over me that, although I now feel utterly useless save as God's child to submit to Him and offer that abandonment for His purposes, He has given me a larger share in effort for Him than I had ever paused to consider. Had there been nothing else, there has been daily Mass with Holy Communion for many years, and in offering the greatest of all sacrifices in union with Christ, and usually mindful of the needs of mankind, I have had a share for which to be very thankful.

I have questioned if it were almost irreverent to be so fascinated by the wording of Holy Writ that I did not give due attention to its teaching.

November 26

I have had untold joy in reading the Bible as I planned. I have used the Douay Version, revised by Bishop Challoner, but have been fortunate in being able to see the original translation made by Gregory Martin, the one "Printed at Doway by Lawrence Kellam at the signe of the holie Lambe M-DC-IX," and also Msgr. Ronald Knox's recent translation.

I have come to a new appreciation of the Douay, and do not long as much as I used to for the sonorous King James Version. Cardinal Newman, brought up on the King James Version, of course, wrote that Challoner winnowed from it, adopted such expressions as suited his needs. His English is that of the middle of the eighteenth century. The language was then rid of many of its excrescences, and had benefited by the simplicity of Addison and Steele, the terseness of Pope, the more practical though less poetical idiom then current. What has interested me most, in addition to the pleasure that I have had in reading different books from end to end without interruption, has been the wealth of expressions that have never been used as book titles. This is a curious admission, and, sometimes as I have read, I have questioned if it were almost irreverent to be so fascinated by the wording of Holy Writ that I did not give due attention to its teachings.

The Bible has been such a usual source for book titles that I have caught myself again and again wondering why combinations of words that struck me as apt had never been employed. Then I remembered that most writers would be unlikely to draw on the Douay. Checking with a King James Concordance and a Catalogue of Books in Print, I found that I had hit on a treasure-trove of possible titles. I had noted before that "a chosen arrow," the expression from *Isaias* employed in the liturgy to describe John the Baptist, was not in the King James Version; but how many more I discovered!

Writers of the nineteenth and twentieth centuries have

been comparatively unacquainted with the so-called Hidden Books, *Ecclesiasticus, Tobias, Judith,* and the rest because these are not in most Protestant Bibles printed since 1826. These, it seems to me, contain lines with as much gist as many in *Proverbs,* and descriptions of nature as lovely as those in the *Canticle of Canticles.*

I have been jotting down a few expressions that appealed to me: "fields of peace," "the wind in his hands," "a ready heart," "the everlasting hills," "success with an angel," and "the voice of a lie." The references to the out-of-doors, to sky, clouds, stars, sun, and moon in *Wisdom* and *Ecclesiasticus* offer a revelation. Rarely, "the wind is still," generally it blows from the north or south or is "a whistling wind." Anyone who has been in Palestine finds its moods evoked by such phrases as "the dark veil of forgetfulness," "stones of trial," "tumult of murmuring," and "the glory of the stars."

I have been thinking of my mother after Andrew was killed at twenty-four in the Battle of the Marne. She had a sort of comfort in the lines in *Wisdom* on a young man's dying, ". . . but the understanding of a man is grey hairs, and a spotless life is old age." I looked that up in the early translation, Gregory Martin's, and I think that those of us who have lived through long searing years ponder it sympathetically: "He was taken away lest malice should change his understanding, or lest anie guile might deceive his soule."

Judith is not a favorite with me. I always resent portions of it being used in the liturgy in reference to the Blessed Virgin. But there is a haunting quality in its language. Judith prayed, when making ready to approach Holofernes, "Let him be caught in the net of his own eyes in my regard." She clothed herself in "the garments of gladness." She "weakened him with the beauty of her face . . . her beauty made his soul her captive." How many souls have been made captive by beauty!

I could go on almost indefinitely on the subject, and I can not resist *Ecclesiasticus:* "the bread of understanding," "the hand of the proud," "peace in his possessions," "sand and salt," "blood of thy soul." Naturally, a person who has seen wreck wrought by unwise generosity is impressed by the verse, "For it is better that thy children should ask of thee than that thou look toward the hands of thy children."

Now, there is nothing outside to disturb the inner silence.

November 27

I shall meditate this Advent on the reasons for the coming of Jesus. He said that He came that we might have life and have it more abundantly. And always He stressed the thought of peace. "On earth, peace," the angels would sing at the time of the Nativity, presaging His constant, "My peace I give you," "Peace be unto you." I wish my soul to be in quiet silence as I prepare for Christmas this year.

Mv mind keeps dwelling on the Antiphon, *Rorate Cœli:* "Drop down dew, ye heavens, from above, and let the clouds rain the Just One: let the earth open and bud forth the Savior." And again and again I repeat in my heart the English carol,

He cam al so stille
  Ther his moder was
As dew in Aprille
  That falleth on the grass.

As we grow older, there is something very special about Advent, for the time of our particular judgment draws near. Faith teaches us to prepare in peace for life eternal. When I was young and had to be busy about many things before Christmas, I took comfort in the lines that begin, "Let my heart the cradle be, Of Thy bleak Nativity." Now, there is nothing outside to disturb the inner silence. This is the best season of the year to be laid up, for I have time to prepare for our Lord's coming.

December 4

Advent may well be one of our most productive seasons spiritually. While we await the coming at Christmas of our Infant Savior, we meditate on our lowliness, accept our nothingness in the scheme of life about us, and remember that, while others are busy with material preparations for the feast, and we more neglected because of their being so occupied, we have leisure to make ready for the ever nearer Vision of God. Lines from the Preface of Christmas take on new meaning, ". . . that while we acknowledge Him as God seen by men, we be drawn by Him to love of things unseen."

Many of the miracles recorded in the Gospels were wrought by Jesus at the request of persons not asking for themselves.

December 7

A measure of calm is restored to all difficult human relations when we are finally convinced that nothing that we do avails, and turn to our Lord, Who loves better than we do. Prayer, such as the unremitting prayer of Monica for Augustine, is our best resource. Once we have given a matter into God's care, we are not inclined to nag or fret or agitate questions. It is a joy to note that many of the miracles recorded in the Gospels were wrought by Jesus at the request of persons not asking for themselves. In dealing with hardened hearts, we have a tremendous advantage psychologically if it is known that we have appealed to a higher court and left our cause there.

God is with each soul in a state of grace, my own little one included.

December 8

The feast of the Immaculate Conception. "The Lord possessed me in the beginning of His ways, before He made anything from the beginning: I was set up from eternity, and of old before the earth was made: the depths were not as yet, and I was already conceived." So runs the verse from *Proverbs* read at Lauds this morning. And at Mass, we read one from *Isaias,* "I will greatly rejoice in the Lord, and my soul shall be joyful in my God; for he hath clothed me with the garments of salvation and with the robe of justice he hath covered me, as a bride adorned with her jewels." It is as if the Church would draw, from the wells of wisdom, thoughts on the wonder of the sinlessness of Mary, showing that, from all time, the idea of perfect grace has captivated men's hearts. Since the doctrine of the Immaculate Conception was promulgated in 1854, the attention of all has been called to the fact that one human person, and one only, has been entirely without the stain of sin. Had our Lady had no other prerogative, this spotlessness would win for her the admiration of mankind.

This is the feast that celebrates the grace of Mary, and truly it is sanctifying grace that is predominant in our minds today. Sanctifying grace, our most precious possession. Perhaps as we age, we, who love grace and see ourselves sinful, are sometimes more troubled than repentant when we consider our faults. We have struggled for so long, and are humanly weary of our weakness. Today, I have been trying to regard my soul peacefully, courageously, serene in the faith that if I but do my part and correspond with the grace that God bestows, He will lead me to the degree of perfection to which I am called. The recognition of my faults is in itself a grace, and accentuates for me my knowledge of my dependence on God. Especially now, when I am so much alone, it is necessary to avoid what might throw my conscience out of focus. I ask our Lady to remind me to preserve the sanctifying grace that I hope is mine whenever I say Gabriel's words, the Offertory of today's Mass: "Hail Mary, full of grace: the Lord is with thee." God is with each soul in a state of grace, my own little one included, and He wishes it a peaceful abode.

*I turn to the Holy Spirit for guidance not
furnished by man, and yield the rest of my
course to Him in entire trust.*

December 12

The snow falls softly. Winter is upon us and I shall be
looking out on the white earth and the snow-laden trees
rather than making snowmen with the children who are
already hastening out to play. I wonder what the winter
will bring. Many months have passed since this journal
was begun in conscious preparation for real old age, and
the recent accident has brought the thought of its immi-
nence nearer. Of its physical handicaps, I have a convincing foretaste.

During the year, I have let myself dwell as calmly as possible on the persisting weaknesses in my character. I am
nearer my *Nunc Dimittis*, and, although lonelier in a
human way for companionship, more conscious that,
deprived of such, the soul depends entirely on God. I turn
to the Holy Spirit for guidance not furnished by man, and
yield the rest of my course to Him in entire trust. A just
estimate of myself will keep me truly humble, and so I will
accept, pray, and love our Lord as His lowly child.

December 16

Glancing back through these pages, I note how frequently I have alluded to the saints who grew to be old.
Of these, John the Evangelist and Philip Neri have been
my own favorites. One belonged to the first days of the
Church, one to that time of new beginning that signaled
the Counter-Reformation. I loved both before I dreamed

that the years might pile up for me as they did for them, but now my affection for them increases. I have been considering St. John today. I wonder if he attracted me originally because he was the Beloved Disciple, "that disciple whom Jesus loved," and if I loved him because Christ did. Perhaps. Anyway, one day I entered a room where Mother and Aunt Lucy were sitting in earnest conversation. They drew me into the talk with the question, "Could you choose but one of the four Gospels, which would you select?" "Saint John's," I answered immediately. They reminded me that had I only that, there would be no account of the Hidden Life, no *Magnificat*, no *Nunc Dimittis*. Nevertheless, that was and remains my choice, for this Gospel, with its stress on the Divinity of Jesus and His warm, human understanding, is very dear to me. Now when my heart seems cold and dry, I turn to the record of the final discourse of Jesus and His prayer for His disciples. When the thought of old age oppresses, I read the last chapter with our Lord's words to St. Peter concerning it, and His answer to Peter's query in John's regard. St. John's record of our Lord's words about himself touch me especially these days:

> . . . So I will have him to remain till I come, what is it to thee? Follow thou me.
> This saying therefore went abroad among the brethren, that that disciple should not die. And Jesus did not say to him: He should not die; but: So I will have him to remain till I come, what is it to thee?

In the long years that followed the Resurrection, John must have wondered many times what our Lord intended. It is said that this Gospel was written after John left

Patmos: if so, he had experienced the Romans' attempt to martyr him at the Latin Gate, and then had worked in the mines on the bleak Mediterranean island of Patmos (my heart thrilled when our small ship skirted it many years ago). Boiling oil and forced labor and all of the trials of age had been his to endure, and still his call had not come. Perhaps he knew that Jesus let him grow old because He trusted His faithfulness, for he alone of all the apostles had stood by the cross on Calvary and been faithful to the last. To me it seems right that one who could be so trusted should remain to link the generations of early Christians. St. John doubtless pondered often the words that he wrote in his Gospel, that Jesus "having loved His own who were in the world, loved them unto the end."

She happened to be where Mary worshipped the Baby Jesus, and I like to think of her there representing all the aged.

December 18

Reading the Scriptures so much these days, my mind harks back again and again to Palestine. One day, when Mother and I were in the Grotto of the Nativity at Bethlehem, the only human being whom I saw was an old, old woman draped in a white woolen shawl. So still that she seemed part of the prevailing silence, the reason for her being there was evident. Probably she could not read the words surrounding the vermilion star fitted into the paving: "HIC DE VIRGINE MARIA JESUS CHRISTUS NATUS EST." One of God's faithful old, she was there because of Jesus, but she might have been in Notre Dame or the

Cathedral of Seville, behind a giant pillar in St. Peter's, or crouched in a hamlet church near a Louisiana bayou. She happened to be where Mary worshipped the Baby Jesus, and I like to think of her there representing all the aged.

While all things were in quiet silence, and the night in the midst of her course, Thy almighty word, O Lord, came from heaven, from Thy royal throne.

December 30

"While all things were in quiet silence, and the night in the midst of her course, Thy almighty word, O Lord, came from heaven, from Thy royal throne."

Glossary

Abbé: Priest.

Acolyte: See "Altar Boys."

Act of 1585: Parliament, alarmed by a plot to kill the Protestant Elizabeth and set the Catholic Mary of Scotland on the throne, passed this act that led to many martyrdoms.

Act of Contrition: A prayer of sorrow for sin. The Act of Contrition familiar to Catholics in the early 1900s was as follows: "O my God, I am heartily sorry for having offended Thee, and I detest all my sins, because of Thy just punishments, but most of all because they offend Thee, my God, who art all-good and deserving of all my love. I firmly resolve, with the help of Thy grace, to sin no more and to avoid the near occasions of sin."

Act of Thanksgiving: Prayer of thanksgiving.

Advent: The first four weeks of the liturgical year, beginning with the Sunday closest to November 30 and ending Christmas eve. A time of looking forward to Christ's Second Advent and to celebrating his Incarnation.

All Saints' Day: A feast day in honor of saints who do not have a special day of honor in the church calendar.

All Souls' Day: A day to commemorate all who have died.

Allocution: Homily or sermon.

Altar Boys: Children who assist the priest during the Mass.

Altar Rail: See "Communion Rail."

Annecy: City in France near Swiss border; home of St. Francis de Sales.

Annunciation: The angel Gabriel's announcement to Mary that she would bear a child (see Luke 1:26-38), celebrated March 25.

Anselm: St. Anselm of Canterbury, ca. 1033-1109; theologian, writer, archbishop.

Antiphons: Short verses used as a refrain with psalms.

Aquinas, Thomas: ca. 1225-74; Dominican theologian and poet known as a Doctor of the Church. Miss Hope calls him "the saint of the Blessed Sacrament" because of his famous hymn, *Adoro te devote* ("I devoutly adore you"). The *Summa* is his massive theological work.

Ash Wednesday: The first day of Lent, marked by fasting and receiving ashes on the forehead as a sign of mortality and repentance.

Assumption: The teaching that Mary, at her death, was taken body and soul to Heaven. Though widely believed for over a thousand years, this has been official Catholic dogma only since 1950.

Athanasian Creed: A fourth- or fifth-century creed that affirms and explains the doctrines of the Trinity and the Incarnation. It is recited on Trinity Sunday.

Augustine: 354-430; Bishop of Hippo (North Africa), theologian, and writer. Considered a Doctor of the Church, he shaped Western theology both Catholic and Protestant. He is commemorated August 28.

Baltimore Catechism: See "Gibbons, Cardinal."

Beatific Vision: Union with God after death, in which the human soul sees, knows, and loves God directly.

Benedicite: The hymn of praise to the God of all creation sung by Daniel's three companions in the fiery furnace. In Catholic versions of Scripture, this is found in Daniel 3:52-90. In separate editions of the apocryphal/deuterocanonical books, it is recorded in verses 29-68 of *The Prayer of Azariah* and *The Song of the Three Jews.*

Benediction: A service of prayer in the presence of the Blessed Sacrament, concluding with a benediction (blessing).

Benedictus: Zechariah's prayer (Luke 1:68-79).

Bernard: St. Bernard of Clairvaux, 1090-1153; abbot, founder of monasteries, preacher of a Crusade, writer, and Doctor of the Church.

Blessed Sacrament: To "visit the Blessed Sacrament" is to go to a church where the consecrated bread (the Host) is kept and to pray in its presence.

Breviary: The book used in observing the Divine Office (now called the Liturgy of the Hours). See "Day Hours" and "Canonical Hours."

Canonical Hours: Set times for reading the Divine Office. Monasteries traditionally observed seven: vespers and compline in the evening; matins and lauds before dawn; and prime, terce, sext, and none at three-hour intervals beginning at sunrise.

Carmelite: Member of a strict religious order that included St. Teresa of Avila, St. John of the Cross, and St. Therese of Lisieux.

Cathedra: The church from which a bishop administers his diocese. The name comes from cathedra, "chair," the bishop's throne.

Catherine of Siena: 1347-80; mystic and adviser of popes; one of two female Doctors of the Church.

Chalice: The cup that holds the wine used in Holy Communion.

Challoner, Bishop: Richard Challoner, 1691-1781; English bishop who studied at Douai and revised the Douay-Rheims Bible.

Chaplets of the Rosary: The Rosary developed as a substitute for the monastic practice of saying all 150 psalms every week. Instead of 150 psalms, the person said 150 prayers, usually the "Hail Mary," while keeping track of them with beads. A chaplet of the Rosary consists of sixty prayers.

Chesterton, Gilbert Keith: 1874-1936; prolific and much quoted English writer who converted to Catholicism in 1922; his works include the Father Brown detective stories, *Orthodoxy*, and biographies of Thomas Aquinas and Francis of Assisi.

Christ the King: The feast of Christ the King is now celebrated in late November, one week before the beginning of Advent.

Ciborium: The container holding the consecrated Hosts (communion bread) that the priest gives to communicants.

Communion Rail: Before Vatican II in the early sixties, a railing separated the sanctuary—the area surrounding the altar—from the nave, where the congregation sat. Worshipers came forward and knelt at the railing to receive communion.

Compline: See "Canonical Hours."

Confession: One of the seven sacraments of the Roman Catholic church, also known as penance; now called the sacrament of reconciliation. During the first half of the twentieth century, devout Catholics went to confession every week.

Confessor: The priest who hears confession and offers God's forgiveness.

Confirmation: A sacrament that includes anointing with oil, the imposition of hands, and a prayer for the indwelling of the Holy Spirit. It was customary to choose a confirmation name in honor of a saint. Children are normally confirmed by the bishop.

Convent of the Visitation: St. Frances de Sales and St. Jeanne de Chantal founded the Visitation order of nuns in 1610.

Cornette: An elaborate headdress worn by the French Sisters of Charity.

Corporal Works of Mercy: Actions that provide for others' physical needs. Traditionally there are seven: feeding the hungry, giving drink to the thirsty, clothing the naked, visiting the imprisoned, sheltering the homeless, visiting the sick, and burying the dead.

*Corpus Christi***:** Latin, "the Body of Christ." A feast day in honor of the Eucharist is celebrated two weeks after Pentecost (nine weeks after Easter).

Counter-Reformation: Sixteenth-century reforms within the Roman Catholic Church, including the Council of Trent, various missionary movements, and renewed interest in spirituality and humanism.

Crucifix: A cross bearing an image of the body of Christ. In most Catholic churches, a large crucifix is in front, behind the altar. A crucifix is also attached to a Rosary. The figure of Jesus on the cross is called a *corpus:* Latin for "body."

Day Hours: Regular times of daily prayer and psalm singing, as practiced in monasteries and by some individuals. Also called the Liturgy of the Hours or the Divine Office.

*De profundis***:** "Out of the depths"—Psalm 130 (or 129).

Decades: A grouping of ten Rosary beads plus one Our Father. A Rosary has five decades, one for each of the Mysteries used for meditation.

Direction: See "Spiritual Direction."

Dismas, Sister: Dismas is the traditional name of the dying thief to whom the crucified Jesus promised a place in Paradise. People in religious life used to take a saint's name when they professed their vows.

Douay Version: The Douay-Rheims Version of the Bible, originally published in 1582 (NT) and 1609 (OT), revised in the eighteenth century, and used by Catholics until the mid-sixties.

Ejaculations: Short prayers, also called "aspirations."

Ember Days: Three days of fasting and abstinence formerly observed in each season of the year.

English College: Seminaries established for English Catholics in exile in Rome, Spain, and France; the students hoped eventually to restore England to Catholicism.

English Martyrs: The approximately 360 Catholics executed by Protestant monarchs during the sixteenth and seventeenth centuries in England. (It should be noted that the English Catholic monarchs executed nearly as many Protestants during the same time period.)

Eustochium: St. Eustochium, who died in about 420, was the daughter of St. Paula. The two women went to Palestine and helped St. Jerome translate the Bible into Latin.

Exaltation of the Holy Cross: Now called "Triumph of the Cross," this feast is celebrated September 14 in honor of the discovery of Christ's cross by Constantine's mother, St. Helena, in 335.

Extreme Unction: The sacramental anointing of the dying, usually preceded by confession and followed by reception of Holy Communion. As a result of the Second Vatican Council (1962-65), the sacrament is now offered, with prayers for healing, to the sick and the aged, not just to the dying. Thus it is no longer called Extreme Unction, but the Anointing of the Sick.

Faber: Frederick W. Faber, 1814-63; English Catholic convert, priest, and writer of books and hymns.

Fast: When this was written, Catholics were required to fast before receiving Communion: no food or drink could be taken after the evening meal until Mass, usually the next morning. An evening Mass shortened the fast. Today the fast has been shortened to one hour and, for the sick and elderly, fifteen minutes.

Feast of the Epiphany: January 6. *Epiphany* is from the Greek for "manifestation." The feast commemorates the visit of the wise men, when Christ was first manifested to the Gentiles.

Fiat: Latin, "Let it be," from Mary's words to the Angel Gabriel: "Here am I, the servant of the Lord; let it be with me according to your word" (Luke 1:38).

Fiat voluntas tua: "Thy will be done."

First Communion: Catholic children normally make their First Communion at age seven, shortly after their first confession (now called reconciliation). Traditionally the children dress in white; the little girls may wear short veils like brides.

First Friday: Many Catholics receive the Eucharist the first Friday of each month. This popular devotion was begun in the seventeenth century by St. Margaret Mary Alacoque, who also promoted devotion to the Sacred Heart of Jesus.

Fisher, John: 1469-1535; English bishop and scholar; beheaded by Henry VIII for opposing the king's supremacy over the English church. Also called St. John of Rochester.

Frances of Rome: 1384-1440; one of the few married female saints with children. She is commemorated March 9.

Francis de Sales: 1567-1622; French bishop, preacher, and writer. He is commemorated on January 24.

Francis of Assisi: ca. 1181-1226; founder of the Franciscans, crusader, mystic, lover of nature.

Franciscan: The popular name for an order of monks founded by St. Francis of Assisi in the thirteenth century. Their official name is Order of Friars Minor.

Gertrude: St. Gertrude of Helfta, called "the Great," ca. 1256-ca. 1302; German nun, mystic, and author of *Revelations* and *Spiritual Exercises.* She is remembered on November 16.

Gibbons, Cardinal: James Gibbons, 1834-1921. Archbishop of Baltimore from 1878 to his death, author of *Faith of Our Fathers,* and sponsor of the Baltimore Catechism, from which children learned Catholic teaching from 1885 until 1965.

Gloria: The angels' song at Christ's birth (Luke 2:14), used as the opening verse for a longer hymn of praise used near the beginning of the Mass.

Golden Legend: A medieval collection of lives of the saints. It contains a legend about a lion that visited the Bethlehem monastery where Jerome lived. Jerome treated the lion's injured paw, and the lion became a trustworthy domestic animal.

Gregory the Great: Gregory I, pope from 590-604; encouraged monasticism and missionaries; improved the liturgy and disciplined the clergy. Influential writer. He was formerly commemorated March 12; he is now remembered on September 3.

Gregory XI: Pope from 1370-78; he reigned in exile in Avignon, France, until 1377 when, yielding to Catherine's entreaties, he returned to Rome.

"Hail Mary": The words used by the Angel Gabriel when he announced the birth of Christ to Mary.

"Hidden Books": Books included in Catholic and Orthodox, but not Protestant, Bibles often called apocryphal ("hidden") or deuterocanonical ("from the second canon").

Holy Eucharist: Holy Communion. The term *Eucharist* is Greek for "thanksgiving."

Holy Father: The pope; in this case, Pius XII.

Holy Souls: Redeemed persons who are still in Purgatory.

Host: The bread used in Holy Communion. The term comes from the Latin *hostia,* or "victim."

Imitation: *The Imitation of Christ,* attributed to Thomas à Kempis. First published in 1472, it is one of the most widely read religious books in the world.

Immaculate Conception: The Roman Catholic teaching that Mary was conceived without original sin. This was declared dogma—an essential teaching of the church—in 1854, just four years before Bernadette's visions (see "Our Lady of Lourdes"). Bernadette had never heard the term until she heard it from the Lady.

Indulgences: God's remission of any punishment that may still be due for a sin that has been sacramentally confessed and absolved. (Indulgences do not remit the eternal punishment due for an unforgiven sin.) An indulgence may be given for prayers or for acts of charity.

Jacopone da Todi: ca. 1230-ca. 1306; Franciscan brother, poet, and hymnwriter.

Jansenist: A seventeenth-century Catholic reform movement stressing human sinfulness. A Jansenist might limit himself to Spiritual Communion out of a feeling of unworthiness to receive the Eucharist.

Jeanne de Chantal: Jeanne Françoise Fremyot, 1572-1641; cofounder with St. Francis de Sales of the Visitation order of nuns.

Jerome: ca. 342-420; St. Jerome, a Father of the Church, was a learned scholar and translator; much of the Latin Vulgate, for centuries the official Bible of the Church, is his work. He is commemorated September 30.

Jesuits: The Society of Jesus, founded by St. Ignatius of Loyola in the sixteenth century and known for its work in foreign missions, spirituality, and education.

Joachim and Anna: The traditional names of Mary's parents, who are unnamed in Scripture. November 21 is the day to commemorate Mary's presentation at the Temple by her parents.

Jogues, Isaac: 1607-46; French Jesuit missionary to North America. One of eight canonized martyrs known as the patron saints of Canada.

John of the Cross: 1542-91; Spanish Carmelite, mystic, reformer, and writer; known especially for *The Dark Night of the Soul.*

[1] From *The Complete Works of St. John of the Cross,* trans. by E. Allison Peers (Newman, Westminster, 1949), p. 110.
[2] *Loc. cit.*

John the Baptist: June 24 is the feast day celebrating the birth of John the Baptist.

Joseph: Husband of the Blessed Virgin Mary. March 19 is St. Joseph's feast day.

Joyful Mysteries: In the Rosary prayer, five Joyful Mysteries are remembered: the Annunciation, the Visitation, the Nativity, the Presentation, and finding Jesus in the Temple. See also "Mysteries."

Judica me: Psalm 43 (or 42).

Jugan, Jeanne: 1792-1879; called Sister Mary of the Cross, founded the Little Sisters of the Poor to help the impoverished elderly.

King James Version: The Authorized Version of the Anglican Church, published in 1611 under James I.

Knox, Monsignor: Ronald Knox, 1888-1957; English Catholic priest who translated the Latin Vulgate into English.

Lauds: See "Canonical Hours."

Lent: The forty days of prayer and fasting before Easter.

Liguori, Alphonsus: 1696-1787; lawyer, bishop, moral theologian, and founder of the Redemptorist order. He is commemorated August 1.

Little Chapter: A short lesson from Scripture intended for reading at one of the canonical hours.

Little Flower: St. Therese of Lisieux.

Little Sisters of the Poor: A religious community founded by Jeanne Jugan (Sister Mary of the Cross) in 1839 in France, dedicated to caring for the elderly.

"Little Way": In her widely read autobiography, St. Therese of Lisieux recommends following the "little way" of becoming as a little child, hoping and trusting in God's mercy.

Liturgical Prayer: Public prayer using prescribed forms.

Louise de Marillac: 1591-1660. French woman who founded the Daughters of Charity (now Sisters of Charity of St. Vincent de Paul).

Loyola, Ignatius: 1491-1556; Spanish nobleman who founded the Society of Jesus (Jesuits), known for their work in foreign missions and education. July 31 is Loyola's memorial day.

Magnificat: Mary's prayer that begins, "My soul magnifies the Lord" (see Luke 1:47-55).

Maid of Orleans: St. Joan of Arc, 1412-1431; burned at the stake after leading a French army against England.

Maître Rossignol: "Maestro nightingale."

Margaret Mary: Margaret Mary Alacoque, 1647-1690; French nun in the Visitation Order who promoted devotion to the Sacred Heart (see "Sacred Heart" and "First Friday"). She is commemorated October 16.

Mary Magdalen: Disciple to whom Jesus first appeared after his resurrection. July 22 is the day on which St. Mary Magdalen is commemorated.

Mary's Shrine: The shrine of Our Lady of Lourdes in the French Pyrenees, to which countless pilgrims have come for healing. See "Our Lady of Lourdes" and "Immaculate Conception."

Maryknoll: The Catholic Foreign Mission Society of America.

Monica: 332-387; the mother of St. Augustine of Hippo. She prayed long and hard for his conversion to Christianity. She is commemorated August 27.

More, Thomas: Author of *Utopia* and Lord Chancellor of England; beheaded by Henry VIII for opposing the king's supremacy over the English church.

Mysteries: The full Rosary of 150 prayers is divided into three chaplets, each of which is accompanied by a meditation. The Joyful Mysteries focus on Christ's Incarnation; the Sorrowful Mysteries, on His death; the Glorious Mysteries, on His resurrection and reign in heaven. See also "Joyful Mysteries."

Neri, Philip: 1515-95; Italian priest who founded religious associations to help the sick and promote holiness.

Newman, Cardinal: John Henry Newman, 1801-90; Anglican priest, scholar, and author who converted to Catholicism in 1845.

None: See "Canonical Hours."

Novena: Prayers and devotions repeated for nine days, often for a specific intention (prayer request).

Novices: Persons who are living in a religious community and preparing to take their first vows.

Nunc Dimittis: Simeon's prayer (Luke 2:29-32).

Offertory: Midway during the Mass, when the bread, wine, and money gifts are brought forward. It is now called the Preparation of the Altar and the Gifts.

Oratory: Societies of priests and brothers dedicated to raising the quality of the priesthood and educating young seminarians. St.

Philip Neri organized the Italian Oratorians in the sixteenth century.

Our Lady of Lourdes: In 1858 Bernadette Soubirous, a fourteen-year-old peasant girl from Lourdes, in southern France, had a series of visions of the Virgin Mary. On March 25, the feast of the Annunciation, Mary told Bernadette, "I am the Immaculate Conception." February 11 is the day dedicated to Our Lady of Lourdes.

Particular Examen: Examining one's conscience and reviewing one's actions, especially before confession.

Pascal: Blaise Pascal, 1623-62; French mathematician and writer. Best known for his *Pensées*, a posthumous collection of notes defending Christianity against Enlightenment thought.

Paul of the Cross: 1694-1775; a visionary, prophet, and healer.

Paula: 347-404; St. Paula was a Roman noblewoman. Widowed young, with five children, she eventually moved to Bethlehem to work with St. Jerome.

Penance: A prayer or action expressing sorrow for sin. See also "Confession."

Penitents: People who come to a priest to confess their sins.

Pentecost: The feast seven weeks (fifty days) after Easter in honor of the coming of the Holy Spirit to the Church (see Acts 2).

Peter: First of the Apostles. June 29 is the feast day of Sts. Peter and Paul.

Pius X: Reigned 1903-1914; canonized (declared a saint) in 1954. At the turn of the century, many Catholics received communion only once a year. Miss Hope thanks him for restoring the practice of frequent—even daily—communion.

Pius XI: Pope 1922-39.

Pius XII: Pope from 1939-1958; in his late seventies at the time of Miss Hope's visit to Rome.

Practice of the Presence of God: The name of a classic book of spirituality written by a seventeenth-century French monastery cook, Brother Lawrence.

Prayer of Reparation: A prayer in which a person joins herself to Christ in order to share in Christ's work of restoring all things to God.

Preface: A prayer that begins the Eucharistic Prayer during the Mass. The Preface varies according to the day and season.

Presentation: Jesus' presentation to the Lord in the Temple, forty days after his birth (see Luke 2:22-40).

Price, Father: Thomas F. Price of Raleigh, North Carolina; with James A. Walsh founded Maryknoll in 1911.

Prime: See "Canonical Hours."

Prudentius: Aurelius Clemens Prudentius, ca. 348-ca. 410; poet and hymnwriter included among the Fathers of the Church.

Psalm 56: Different Bible versions number the psalms differently. In the Douai version, the reference is to Psalm 56:8; in the New American Bible, Psalm 57:8; and in the New Revised Standard Version, Psalm 57:7.

Purgatorio: The second part of Dante's fourteenth-century masterpiece, *The Divine Comedy.*

Purgatory: A place or state of purging, or washing, that prepares redeemed sinners for entry into heaven.

Quinquagesima Sunday: The Sunday that is fifty days before Easter.

Quo vadis: Latin, "Where are you going?" According to legend, Peter fled Rome during a time of persecution. On the Appian Way, he met Jesus. "Where are you going?" Peter asked his Lord. "Back to Rome," said Jesus. So Peter turned around and followed him—to martyrdom.

Quod facis...: "Do quickly what you are going to do." Jesus' words to Judas at the Last Supper, recorded in John 13:27.

Real Presence: The presence of Christ's body and blood in the Eucharist under the form of bread and wine.

Religious: Term used for those who have taken vows of poverty, chastity, and obedience and who live in community; monks (brothers) and nuns (sisters).

Rosary Beads: Used in prayers—the Hail Mary, the Lord's Prayer, and the Doxology—accompanied by meditations on the life of Christ and his mother. See also "Chaplets of the Rosary," "Decades," "Joyful Mysteries," and "Mysteries."

Rose of Lima: 1586-1617; mystic and recluse.

Rule: The way of life outlined for a religious order.

S'adapter...: To adapt one's stride to God's.

Sacraments: Roman Catholics recognize seven sacraments: baptism, the Eucharist, confirmation, marriage, holy orders (ordination), reconciliation, and anointing of the sick. When possible, dying Catholics receive three sacraments: confession (reconciliation), extreme unction (anointing of the sick), and communion.

Sacred Heart: Christ's heart, a symbol of His love. Devotion to the Sacred Heart, with special liturgies, became very popular in the nineteenth century.

Sacristan: The person who cares for a church's liturgical items, such as altar linens and vestments.

Saint-Lazare: The headquarters of the Lazarists, or Vincentians, an order founded by St. Vincent de Paul. Saint-Lazare was originally a leprosarium.

Seven Dolors: September 15 is the memorial of Our Lady of Sorrows. Her seven sorrows ("dolors") are Jesus' circumcision, the flight into Egypt, losing Jesus at the Temple, seeing Jesus on the way to the cross, Jesus' crucifixion, taking Jesus' body down from the cross, and Jesus' burial.

Sevenfold Gifts: A traditional list of gifts of the Spirit based on Isaiah 11:2-3: wisdom, understanding, counsel, fortitude, knowledge, piety, and fear of the Lord.

Sext: See "Canonical Hours."

Sheehan, Canon: Patrick Augustine Sheehan, 1852-1913; Irish novelist and priest.

Sherwin, Ralph: One of the forty English Martyrs canonized (declared a saint) in 1970.

Sinlessness of our Lady: The Roman Catholic church teaches that the Holy Spirit preserved Mary from sin so that she would be a fit mother of God the Son. See "Immaculate Conception."

Sister Sacristan: The sister in charge of liturgical objects used in the Mass.

Sisters of Charity: A religious order dedicated to helping the poor and sick.

Sisters of the Good Shepherd: A religious community founded in France in 1641, dedicated to caring for and evangelizing young women in trouble.

Sistine Chapel: Known for its paintings by Michelangelo, this is the main chapel in the Vatican and the place where cardinals meet to elect a new pope.

Southwell, Robert: 1561-95, Jesuit poet and martyr, canonized (declared a saint) in 1970.

Spiritual Communion: Recognizing one's strong desire to receive communion when one is unable to do so physically.

Spiritual Direction: Prayer and counsel, often in preparation for confession.

Spiritual Director: A priest, religious, or layperson who prays and counsels with people, especially to prepare them for the sacrament of penance (reconciliation).

Spiritual Works of Mercy: Actions that provide for others' spiritual and emotional needs. Traditionally there are seven: admonishing the sinner, instructing the ignorant, counseling the doubtful, comforting the sorrowful, bearing wrongs patiently, forgiving all injuries, and praying for the living and the dead.

Stations: The Stations of the Cross. In Roman Catholic churches, fourteen scenes from Christ's suffering and death are displayed. To "make the Stations" is to pray while contemplating each scene. Also called the Way of the Cross.

Stigmata: Bodily wounds like those received by Christ at the crucifixion, usually received during a mystical experience.

Tabernacle: A container in which the consecrated bread (the Host) is kept.

Terce: See "Canonical Hours."

Teresa: St. Teresa of Avila, 1515-82; mystic, reformer of monasteries, and writer; one of two female Doctors of the Church. She is commemorated October 15.

Therese: Therese of Lisieux, 1873-1897; French Carmelite nun known affectionately as "the Little Flower." St. Therese was formerly commemorated on October 3; her memorial has been moved to October 1.

Thompson, Francis: 1859-1907; English Roman Catholic poet best-known for his poem on conversion, "The Hound of Heaven" (1893).

Transfigured: See Matthew 17:1-8. August 6 is the feast of the Transfiguration.

Transubstantiation: The medieval philosophical explanation of how the bread and wine of the Eucharist become the body and blood of Jesus Christ.

Trinity Sunday: The Sunday after Pentecost.

Veni...: The opening lines of a thirteenth-century hymn: "Come, Holy Spirit, and send forth from heaven the radiance of Thy light." Traditionally sung on the feast of Pentecost just before the reading of the Gospel.

Vianney, Jean: 1786-1859; French parish priest, a gifted confessor; people came from all over Europe to have him pray for them. He is commemorated August 4.

Vicar Apostolic: An office similar to that of bishop, but the territory governed is not yet a diocese, perhaps because of insufficient funds or lack of clergy. Gibbons held this office in North Carolina from 1868 to 1872.

Vincent de Paul: 1581-1660. French priest who devoted his life to helping the poor and is the patron of charitable societies.

Visitation: Mary's visit to Elizabeth while both women were pregnant (see Luke 1:39-56). See also "Convent of the Visitation."

Visits: See "Blessed Sacrament."

Vulgate: The Latin version of Scripture; much of it was translated by St. Jerome.

Ward, Maisie: Cofounder with her husband, Frank Sheed, of the Catholic publishing house Sheed & Ward in 1929.

"While . . . throne.": The quotation is from the deuterocanonical book of Wisdom 18:14-15. It is used as the Entrance Antiphon for the Mass of December 30.

White Dress and Veil: See "First Communion."